Dear J

Universal Basic Income – For and Against

by Antony Sammeroff

You are bringing
beauty into people's
homes!

Maybe you can dream
us up some more effective
tactics, Macheavelli!
We need to win this somehow!

Very Warmly,
Antony

AVR 2025

First published in 2019 by Rational Rise Press, Australia.

Copyright © Antony Sammeroff 2018, 2019, 2020

Cover artwork design by Timothy Virkkala

Layout & Text by James Fox Higgins.

First Printing: 2019

National Library of Australia
Cataloguing-in-Publication data:

Sammeroff, Antony, 1986-
Universal basic income - for and against.

ISBN-13: 978-1-7974542-4-5

ISBN-10: 1-7974-5424-2

RATIONAL RISE PRESS
Australia

www.therationalrise.com

Universal Basic Income – For and Against

by Antony Sammeroff

Foreword by Robert P. Murphy, PhD.
Afterword by Dominic Frisby
Cover by Timothy Virkkala

Dedicated to the End of Poverty.

Moral. Spiritual. Material.

Preface

Thank you for taking the time to read my short book. Texts that you can read in a couple hours are all the rage these days, so I've tried to keep it tight for you. At average speed you can kill it in one sitting if you're persistent. I suggest you read it once or twice then come back to it as a reference manual whenever you get embroiled in a Facebook debate or YouTube comment fight. (It's good to have some copy and paste material, right? Save your time and mental health. You can download the PDF of the first edition from www.beyourselfandloveit.com/ubi). For now, get yourself a hot drink, and enjoy.

This book was originally based upon a talk which I gave at an event in December 2016.[1] I added material from other articles I have written concerning poverty reduction, living standards, automation and the role of government in the economy, then stitched it all together with plenty of new research and writing. If I were a Classic Rock band this would be like the reunion tour where I play all the greatest hits from my famous album, throw in some lesser known tunes to keep the diehards happy, and sneak in the latest material hoping that no one throws a bottle at me. However, though more controversial, you won't be groaning in lament at 'the new stuff'. In my opinion it adds more clarity and depth to the original talk (which you can watch online if you're one of those fans who likes to know the words

---

[1] December 2016, hosted by Johnny Cypher at Fika Cafe in the West End of Glasgow.

to the songs before you see the show. Just type *Scottish Liberty Podcast Universal Basic Income: For and Against* into YouTube.)

Now. I should preface the forthcoming statement by admitting that it takes a certain kind of weirdo to hold a French Economist from the 19th century up as one of their heroes... but my hero – Frédéric Bastiat – wrote a book called *Economic Sophisms* in which he did much the same kind of thing as I do; that is, to try and explain the unintended consequences of well-intentioned economic policies to a lay audience with an occasional spark of humour. And he wrote, in the introduction to that book, "We must admit, that our opponents have a marked advantage over us. They only need a few words to set forth a half-truth; whereas, in order to show that it is a half-truth we must have recourse to long and dry dissertations." I have done everything in my power to avoid turning this little treatise into an arid dissertation of the kind we're all familiar with from school, if not from uni. (Yes, including labouring it with this painfully try-hard 'hip and casual' intro.) Hopefully we'll soon be seeing that, as a consequence, learning a little about economics is what all the cool kids are doing these days and that we're spearheading a new movement. Geek is chic.

I have tried to keep the tone casual while being rigorous with my arguments and evidences and maintaining intellectual integrity. The voice may be more conversational than an academic work, but the material presented is not 'light'. This is not a work of 'pop economics'. You're not 'faking it' if you read this book rather than something from Oxford University Press or whatever; you're getting the real stuff. I would never patronise you. I believe even the most complex concepts in economics can be made readily understandable to the kind of person who would be interested in reading about them, if only they are communicated in a simple, interesting, and even passionate manner. This is necessary if we are ever to redeem this field from its characterisation as "the dismal science". I have a certain advantage over most economists in this respect in that I've reviewed over 150 plays and written a self-help book.[2] That means I have some considerable experience in condensing many observations into a few words and presenting them to a popular audience. That being said, my approach isn't new. The originators of the discipline, such as Adam Smith (hailing from Scotland, like me), Jean-Baptiste Say, David Ricardo, Thomas Malthus and J. S. Mill did not fill their treatises with confusing graphs and unintelligible mathematical equations. They set forth their theories and arguments in the plainest language they could muster, for everyone to read, not just those who were in the exclusive club.

This is for everyone to read, regardless of their familiarity with economic study. Whenever we find agreement, and wherever we disagree, my lines of thinking should appear rational and clear to understand. Therefore, if I present any errors they will be simple to refute as they are not hidden behind

---

[2] It's called *Procrastination Annihilation* and you can download it for free from www.beyourselfandloveit.com/doit.

obscure language or ambiguous terms.

I hope this monograph will give a relatively fresh perspective on the Universal Basic Income debate which is very contemporary and lively at the moment. In fact, I'm sure that spirited rebuttals are bound to follow its release, so please stay up to date with me on my economics blog – which you can find at www.seeingnotseen.blogspot.co.uk; you can also check out the *Scottish Liberty Podcast* which I co-host on YouTube or listen through your podcasting app. We'll see if we can get to the bottom of all this.

Warmly,

Antony Sammeroff.
February 28th, 2018,
March 25th and December 23rd, 2019

Contents

List of Tables, Graphs, Figures and Other Cool (Not-boring!) Economisty Stuff.

Foreword *by Robert P. Murphy, PhD.*

The calls for a default payment from the central government to each citizen (or perhaps each adult) have been around for decades, though sometimes they went by different names. Terms such as a "negative income tax" (championed by Milton Friedman, of all people) or a "basic income guarantee" (which yields the convenient acronym BIG) convey the same general idea as a "universal basic income" or UBI, which is the name adopted in the present booklet.

UBI proposals enjoy surprising support from both the traditional left *and* right. Those on the left view a UBI as the natural extension of the logic of the welfare state. Rather than addressing each potential need in isolation—with separate programs for food, housing, education, childcare, healthcare, job training, and even free computer/internet access (provided in libraries and other community centres)—why not simplify matters and admit that the government is going to guarantee a certain floor in living standards, *period*, and get it over with? After all, that's ultimately what motivates public support for the piecemeal programs. If nothing else, a *universal* income program would remove the stigma currently attached to existing "welfare" programs.

On the right, support for a UBI is admittedly more tepid, but it is tangible—and growing. Although they acknowledge the potential dangers, a small but vocal portion of libertarian and conservative thinkers (at least in U.S. politics) have been pushing some form of a UBI as the only politically feasible way to reform the welfare state in a pro-growth fashion. *Given* that the central government is currently spending enormous sums in paternalistic programs that often deaden the incentive to work, so the argument goes, wouldn't a UBI be far preferable?

I must confess that I ignored UBI proposals until quite recently. Given the American propensity to reject "socialism" out of hand, I thought that whatever the possible merits of UBI, *surely* the American public would never support such an explicit scheme for direct handouts from the federal government, given regardless of need on the part of the individual.

Well, I was wrong. The Medicare program, of course, is a "universal" healthcare support for the elderly, regardless of need. And with the passage of the Affordable Care Act (a.k.a. "Obamacare"), the conversation has shifted such that calls for a so-called Public Option and even Single Payer are no longer considered signs of Russian radicalism. Indeed, the (failed) presidential primary bid of Bernie Sanders, along with the successful 2018 Democratic Party primary run (for the U.S. Congress as a representative from New York state) of Alexandria Ocasio-Cortez, have served to *put socialism back on the table* in U.S. politics.

Furthermore, the possibilities of driverless cars and other applications of AI—especially in the context of a "jobless recovery" in which the official unemployment rate is at rock-bottom levels while many young people still aren't working—as well as the ongoing trends of globalization, have caused Americans but also other advanced countries to worry about the segment of their populations who *aren't* particularly adept at website design or other niches in the New Economy.

Along with academics and policy wonks, we also have popular billionaires—such as Mark Zuckerberg and Elon Musk—offering various shades of support for UBI, saying it is the only way to cope with the coming wave of automation.[3]

In this context, I was pleased to learn of Antony Sammeroff's booklet on UBI. Like it or not, this issue is *not* going away, and the public should start mulling it over more seriously *before* the major economies suffer another major recession. (This is something that I personally believe is inevitable, given the unprecedented actions of the Federal Reserve, Bank of England, ECB, Bank of Japan, and other central banks in the wake of the financial crisis of 2008.)

Sammeroff's contribution is a very readable introduction to the major issues in the debate. This makes his booklet fairly unique, in that most other writings are either strongly *for* or *against* UBI. Yet as the very title of the present volume makes clear, in the following pages you will see *both* sides of the argument. Furthermore, Sammeroff is *fair* to both sides, because his own views have evolved over time. So he doesn't

---

[3] See for example Catherine Clifford, "What billionaires and business titans say about cash handouts in 2017," CNBC article, December 28, 2017, available at: https://www.cnbc.com/2017/12/27/what-billionaires-say-about-universal-basic-income-in-2017.html.

construct strawman arguments, but instead sincerely explains the ostensible virtues of UBI, but also warns of its potential downsides.

Finally, I was very pleased to see that Sammeroff offers other solutions to alleviate the plight of the poor. "You can't beat something with nothing," as they say. If there are serious problems with a UBI, it's not enough to point them out. We must also show that there are more practical ideas that can achieve at least some of the goals of the pro-UBI camp.

My own bit of advice to the reader is this: Before embracing UBI based merely on its abstract principles, *insist on an actual numerical proposal*. As Sammeroff explains, there is a trade-off involved: The more people who benefit from a UBI by (say) being able to care for a sick relative, or to pursue a career as an artist, while still enjoying a respectable standard of living, it necessarily means that everybody else in the conventional work force must have a greater share of their pay taken in taxes.

Whether you end up *For* or *Against* UBI, I am sure you will benefit from Sammeroff's breezy yet thoughtful discussion.

Robert P. Murphy
Research Assistant Professor
Free Market Institute at Texas Tech
July 28, 2018

Universal Basic Income – For and Against

The idea of a *Universal Basic Income* provided by the government to each and every citizen as a right has been gaining in popularity as an alternative to the current economic system and welfare state. On the face of it, it has an appeal to both the left, who want to ensure that everyone's basic needs are met, and to the right, who want to preserve a market economy rather than see it gradually replaced by central planning and outright socialism. Even some economic libertarians who consider themselves neither left nor right but are decidedly for smaller government have come out in favour of it. Matt Zwolinski of *Bleeding Heart Libertarians,* and Michael Munger, former chair of the political science department at Duke University, and author of *Tomorrow 3.0: Transaction Costs and the Sharing Economy* (2018), whom I had a spirited but friendly debate with on the *Lions of Liberty* podcast following the original release of this book on kindle.[4]

The conservative political scientist Charles Murray, who received considerable criticism (as well as praise) for his controversial book *Losing Ground: American Social Policy 1950–1980,* has since advocated for the UBI as an alternative to the current welfare system. *Losing Ground*, released in 1984, not only critiqued the failures of the American welfare state, but charged it with increasing poverty by rewarding short-sighted behaviour which prevented people from escaping it.

---

[4] You can listen to the debate at:
https://soundcloud.com/scottishliberty/ubidebate.

The economist and free-market advocate Milton Friedman also advocated a species of UBI in the form of the *negative income tax*, where people earning below a certain amount receive supplemental pay from the government as a "top up" instead of paying taxes, which he posited as a superior alternative to the current welfare system for reasons we will soon discuss.

In this little book I mean to explore the merit of arguments both in favour and against the UBI, and spark off some thoughts on various alternative approaches to tackling poverty and meeting everyone's needs. For those who remain in favour of the Universal Basic Income I hope it will make your thinking more robust, bring certain problems to your attention so that you can solve them, and help you supplement your platform with some additional policies that will make the scheme more feasible. For those who are against, I hope it will help crystallise your objections into a concrete platform that stands *for* something – not just *against* the UBI. It is always preferable to offer a strong, practical, and plausible alternative to a policy than simply dismiss it. That is, if you wish to capture the public imagination, satisfy people's desire to work for positive change, and reach widespread appeal. Everybody wants progress, and hopefully, regardless of which side of the debate we land on, we can find agreement on at least a few things that would be a step in the right direction.

Here's to common ground!

I first heard of the UBI as an alternative to the current

welfare system over a decade ago in a book released in 1990 so the idea has certainly been knocking around for a while. I instantly became a convert, convinced that it was an idea that would improve upon the current system without any appreciable drawbacks. I even made a YouTube video to promote the idea myself in 2008. But there was not much talk or recognition of the proposal at the time. In fact, it was not until more recently that it has risen in the public consciousness.

The idea is that every man, woman and possibly child (through their parent or guardian, as a replacement for child benefit) is entitled to a certain amount of money from the state – regardless of their income. Not a huge sum of money, but enough to ensure that our basic needs are met and that no one will go hungry. The simplest proposal is that the government simply deposits the sum into each person's bank account every month. In an alternative rendering, people who are not earning or are on low incomes receive their basic income as a direct payment, while those with high earnings receive it in the form of a tax deduction. People in between might receive a mixture of both.

Most benefits, pensions, tax allowances and social security payments would be replaced by this scheme, leading to a simplification of the welfare system and a drop in administrative costs.

It's easy to see the appeal...

For

- It would make sure that everyone's fundamental needs were met.

- It would do away with poverty traps where if people earn more, they will actually take home less because they will lose some or all of their benefits. Economists have spotted what they call "welfare cliffs" where, for example, if someone does more than 16 hours of paid work, they might lose housing benefits, free trips to the optician, food stamps or a multitude of other benefits, which – once aggregated – lead them to being less well-off for working more. Someone choosing to work more hours and become of more use to others is likely to fall (or rather, be thrown,) off the welfare cliff. This herds people into permanent dependence on handouts.

Under the UBI, whatever people are paid for working would be given to them *in addition to* their basic income. This would remove the disincentive to work. There would always be a benefit to contributing more to society as people would always have something to gain from taking up more hours.

- It would remove perverse incentives where on one side you have unemployed people who want to work, and on the other, jobs that need doing, but no one doing those jobs because the pay for the work is less than what they can receive on benefits.

- It would allow people who are underemployed or in low-paid positions to supplement their income.

- It would remunerate people who engage in voluntary

work such as care work, child care, and care for the elderly, much of which currently goes unpaid for. More people might even start volunteering and helping the needy as they would not have to sacrifice making a living to do so.

- It would recognise the contributions of women (and sometimes men) as home-makers who would gain an income independent of their partners or spouse for the work they do that goes unpaid. It is also worth mentioning that much of the care work and volunteering which goes unremunerated is done by women, this would monetarily acknowledge them for contributions that currently go unpaid.

- On a related point, the benefits to the development of a child of one (or both) parents staying home from work for longer after their birth are numerous and well established. The UBI would make it easier for families to prioritise the care and maturation of their newborn if they chose to do so.

- It would simplify the complex array of benefits including pensions, tax allowances, working tax credits, child benefit and social security payments into one scheme which would be less bureaucratic and cheaper to administrate than the current system.

- It may also reduce government outgoings on law enforcement if it leads to a drop in poverty-driven crime.

- It could significantly alleviate stress, which is

considered to be one of the greatest killers of the modern age. We may see a huge reduction in stress-related illnesses and other conditions if people did not live in fear of losing their homes or going hungry should they become unemployed for any reason. This, in turn, would save the government money on healthcare expenditure.

- Some have gone as far as to claim that the UBI would reduce domestic violence and child abuse by reducing financial stress and other sources of conflict. It would certainly offer a clear way out to those who are in unhappy relationships, even if they have been out of the labour market for many years and missed the opportunity to learn skills that would help them support themselves on their own.

- Research has shown that people in straits of economic insecurity have a reduced cognitive ability equal to 13 IQ points.[5] Advocates claim that, therefore, the UBI would help people make smarter decisions, and facilitate them in improving their own situation by providing the security they need to focus on their families and other priorities.

- It would encourage entrepreneurship by giving people the security to take the risk of becoming self-employed or starting a business.

- It would allow people to improve their prospects by

[5] Anandi Mani, A., Mullainathan, S., Shafir, E., Zhao, J. (2013) *"Poverty Impedes Cognitive Function"*, Science, Vol. 341, Issue 6149, pp. 976-980

taking time out of the workforce to retrain for a different job.

- It might improve the work environment for employees in general if people, faced with poor bosses or conditions, could walk away from their positions with relative security. Employers may be put under pressure to reform hostile, unpleasant, or needlessly stressful workplaces.

- From the conservative side, many labour laws and regulations might therefore become unnecessary and could be abandoned, cutting the red tape, and unnecessary expenditure on monitoring compliance from businesses and government departments.

- Also, from the conservative side, many services which are currently provided by the state may be deemed affordable to all once a basic income scheme is instituted. That would allow them to be placed back on the market, for competition and increased efficiency through private provision. As one prominent advocate put it, "The government might not be good at much, but one thing it does seem to do reliably is write people cheques."

- Since people would be given their basic income directly to spend it as they please, it would preserve the market economy relative to more intrusive forms of government assistance or central planning, where officeholders and bureaucrats attempt to organise production "on behalf of the poor" (or "the workers" or "the people") leading to a disastrous misallocation of resources and authoritarian dictatorship.

- In the wake of widespread automation and the advance of Artificial Intelligence, more and more entry-level jobs appear to be disappearing, and a Universal Basic Income will ensure that those displaced by machines and computers do not find themselves destitute. I dedicate a whole section to evaluating this claim later in the book because it is such a critical point to address.

- It would remove the stigma of people who are on benefits as being "parasites" since everyone would be receiving the same treatment. Even if you are a high earner you would still be receiving your basic income – either as a direct payment or a tax deduction.

- Most countries currently face a demographic shift in the age of their population which threatens to force a diminishing percentage of working-age people into supporting an increasing number of elderly and infirm retirees. The UBI would not only make sure the elderly have a regular and reliable sum of money coming in, but make it easier for people to save for their retirement.

It does sound compelling. It certainly seems to promise some significant benefits over the current welfare system. It would probably still yield its fair share of problems and abusers, but of course those exist under the present system as well so that's nothing new. If anything, even while imperfect, it is surely bound to be vulnerable to less corruption than the bureaucratic nightmare which is the present system.

All of this said, the more I have come to learn about economics, and after over ten years of study I am *still* learning more about economics,[6] the more I have come to see that economics is not so much about the immediate and apparent effects of any policy, but its knock-on effects which will not necessarily be intuitively predictable at a glance. A classic article on this very point was written by the French economist Frédéric Bastiat around 1849, entitled *That Which is Seen and That Which is Not Seen,* and is freely available online.

It's actually a very elegant subject. I began to write a blog in 2016 in hope of demonstrating that, which you can follow if you feel moved to learn more. I attempt to explain these concepts in a way that I think anyone would be interested in and understand.[7]

Economics is founded on the perception that every policy provides incentives and disincentives, and that

---

[6] I find the subject fascinating, although I must confess that the field has done little to redeem itself of the moniker, "the dismal science". In its academic form, economics has now become so full of impenetrable charts and advanced mathematics that even many bright people cannot cope with its demands. This is despite the fact that the originators of the field, such as Adam Smith, managed to write landmark treatises like *The Wealth of Nations* lucidly, comprehensibly, and even artistically without including a single graph or equation. Underlying his writing was a basic humanism and positive regard for man and his prospects. This ethos is something I would desperately like to see return to our currently polemical and often vicious political discourse.

[7] If you want to learn more you can find my blog at www.seeingnotseen.blogspot.co.uk.

those affect people's behaviours. A grounding in economics allows you to follow a train of logic to anticipate what some of the unexpected consequences of any policy might be. That's what I find fascinating about it. It's an extremely useful skill and it helps you make better sense of the world.

Now, perhaps I'm not going to make myself the most popular person in the discussion by talking about some of the potential drawbacks of pursuing the Universal Basic Income as a policy. But don't shoot the messenger! Because good ideas are anti-fragile. If a good idea is challenged and it is able to sustain itself, then it can only be strengthened and become more robust. If it cannot sustain the challenge, then perhaps it wasn't such a good idea in the first place. So, let's talk about some of the potential hazards of the Universal Basic Income scheme, and then we will round off with some simple policies that would increase living standards – especially for the poor. In my view at least some of these policies would need to be adopted as a prerequisite to the adoption of a Universal Basic Income for reasons that will become clear.

Against

- I completely agree with UBI advocates that many people will still do productive work even if all their basic needs are taken care of, and they are given money to take care of them. However, it's worth keeping in mind that when you get a job – when someone pays you for something – they're paying you for work which is of service to others. Otherwise, they wouldn't bother paying you. Obviously you're doing something for someone that they value, which is why they give you a wage.

A lot of the work that might be done under a Universal Basic Income may have some value, but it may not be the full value that paid work provides to other members of society. And what you are going to have to some degree – however large or small you think that degree may be – is a trade-off between people who are pursuing their personal interests and hobbies (however worthy), and people who are working in jobs that everyone else is enjoying the benefit of. The people who are doing the *necessary* work will have to admit lower standards of living to subsidise those who are pursuing leisure, even although they are the ones doing the heavy lifting.

It's worth mentioning that we all benefit from the work that people did before we were even born over and above what they consumed. People produced more than they needed, especially over the last two or three centuries, and they built our bridges and our railways; our roads and the machines that create all the lovely conveniences we enjoy. They created all the great literature and all the scientific advancements. And I fear, that a lot of that work will not be getting done. With less incentive for people to take on less pleasant work, less will be produced, and because of that there will be less to go around for everyone to enjoy.

To summarise that point in economic terms, market transactions select for producers that are providing services that are in demand by whereas a Basic Income does not.

People respond to economic incentives and change their behaviour when government policies change. A drop-off in the amount of productive work done, coinciding with an increase in the number of people living off of that work would be the likely result of the incentives provided by the UBI. This would result in less wealth being created to go around.

- Another might be that employers will see that people do not need the wage they are getting to live on any more, thanks to their basic income, and slash wages. This is tantamount to the government subsidising private companies, shovelling money from the public purse into corporate profits. The company keeps the money from the sale of items, even though the tax-payer has footed the labour costs. This can only lead to more people doing work that is of lesser value, but now easy to pay for thanks to government money, and with it, less of the work that people value most and that really needs doing.[8]

---

[8] Following the original release of this book on kindle, the esteemed Gene Epstein (former economics editor at Barron's Magazine) strongly disputed

- With less being produced, the price of what *is* produced is liable to rise in accordance with the laws of supply and demand. The basic income may soon become inadequate, leading for calls for increases which – if pursued – will escalate the tax rate on those who are doing the paid work, disincentivising the paid work further. This may lead into a vicious circle.

If we return to one of the stated virtues of the Universal Basic Income Scheme – that it would eliminate poverty

---

this argument. While himself an opponent of the UBI, he wrote to say, "The standard Marxist line is that workers need a job, because without one they will starve. Therefore, the 'greedy' capitalist has the upper-hand in labour relations and will always pay workers as little as they can get away with." By this logic, if workers have a stable income from the government, then they can actually hold out for higher wages and reject jobs that don't pay enough to satisfy them. I believe the colloquial expression is "having F-you money"; meaning enough to tell an individual or organization to go to hell without fear of personal repercussions for it.

In economics, the notion that real wages always tend toward the minimum wage necessary to sustain the life of employees has been called "The Iron Law of Wages". This notion has been thoroughly debunked by the evidence of history. Since the time of Marx we have seen truly incredible increases in the living standards of those at the bottom of the economic ladder (as we will discuss in more detail later.) It is also in opposition to more widely accepted notion that wages, like all prices, are arrived at by the laws of supply and demand. Marxists may think that employers get to set the salaries of their employers, but this is not actually the case. If it were everyone would be on minimum wage! Wages are arrived at by supply and demand. The more widely desired someone's talents are the higher they are likely to get paid. For example, a highly proficient computer programmer may have a choice between many attractive positions. On the other hand, people who can do low skilled work are in relatively abundant supply, so they earn a lower wage. These incentives are to entice people to develop skills that are greatly sought after so they can leave poorly paid professions that are overpopulated. Perhaps then, the debate over whether the UBI will raise wages or lower them is void because the value of the task will ultimately be arrived at via supply and demand.

traps where if some people earn more they will lose their benefits and therefore be taking home less – there is also a corollary effect. That is, that in order to pay for this basic income, we must stipulate that when people *do* start earning we will have to see a huge percentage of their income being taxed to pay for it. If you are going to give people 8 or 10 or 12 or 16 grand a year, people who are highly qualified, such as doctors or surgeons, will probably not want to work long hours to be taxed at 70, 80, 90% as standard. They are likely to cut back on hours, decreasing the availability of critical services and (by the laws of supply and demand) increasing the cost of those services. Because it takes a long time to train in these kinds of professions, it will not be easy to fill the gap quickly. Plus, the prestige associated with these professions will soon diminish if the rewards of the job are not seen to adequately reward their demands – including the cost and time invested in many years of education to qualify for them.

If we look at some of the figures behind this, there are about 66.5 million people in the UK. Even at £8k per adult, which is just under the current cost of the UK pension, and pretty much the lowest I can envision someone getting by on (allowing for what passes for some comfort nowadays) you're still looking at £425bn a year to fund the basic income scheme. To put this in context, total government spending this year (2019) is projected at £841 billion, so that amounts to almost half of what our government is spending in total in order to pay for a Universal Basic Income that is absolutely minimal. Many advocates propose figures far exceeding eight thousand pounds.

Now this is not the full story yet of course, because you'd be able to replace most of the current welfare bill. But that only amounts to £240bn – about half the price of the scheme, so you would have to make up the money somehow. The rich don't actually have that kind of cash stowed away in Swiss Bank Accounts to pay for it. The combined wealth of all the billionaires in Britain wouldn't cover the scheme for an entire year. The combined wealth of *all the billionaires in the world* ($8.7 trillion, according to *Forbes)* would only cover a Universal Basic Income of $1000 a month in America for about two and a half years. So, the tax burden will have to be spread across everyone who is working.

One proposal is to put a sales tax on goods in the shops but that amounts to making everything more expensive, so you are basically charging people more for products which you then give back to them as a UBI. Why not just make the UBI smaller to save shuffling the money back and forth? Sales taxes are also considered to be regressive because they hit people on low incomes harder than people on high-incomes. They make it more costly to afford a comfortable lifestyle.

Some leap to the idea of taxing "corporations instead of individuals" to pay for it. But, taxes on corporations will ultimately be paid by the people in general rather than "greedy capitalists". This is because a corporation will have to account for the additional tax burden somehow, and broadly speaking there are three ways they can do it. One is to raise the prices of their products, so you and I pay; another is to not take so many risks, not employ more people, not to expand as much – the workers might not get pay-rises, and the economy might not grow to the same extent. The third way is, of course, that the shareholders go away with less profit. Many might well be in favour of that. It seems that investors just put up the capital in the first place and so they're gaining money for doing little, but what do they do with that money once they are paid their dividends? They're going to invest it in other businesses and machines and factories, that create things, pushing down the cost of consumer goods so we all benefit from cheaper products and a higher standard of living. Remove the incentive and they might just decide to invest in something like property instead, pushing up house prices and rental fees for the rest of us. I'm not saying that's the end of the story, but I mean to point out that every policy has a trade-off – so it's not like when you tax corporations that money just comes out of thin air! It's coming out of other places in the economy where it might already be doing productive work.

Big corporations can afford lawyers and accountants and lobbyists to help them avoid paying taxes, whereas small companies can't. And then when you factor in the fact that you and I pay taxes on our income and spend the rest, but corporations pay tax on what is left after they spend, high corporation taxes create a huge incentive to turn board meetings into trips to Hawaii, consultations into restaurant dinners, and put their cars through as business expenses. It creates waste. That's why when you go to some of these corporations they have lavish lobbies with fountains and gold bannisters, because all of that is tax deductible, and it might seem irresistible to throw the cash at things that look nice rather than give it to the government to spend instead![9]

Bear in mind many corporations are only running on a profit margin of 8-12%. Restaurants and cafes often survive on a profit margin of only three or four percent! So you can't tax them indefinitely. Everything has a trade-off. Most pensions are invested in the stock market as well, so when you "tax corporations" you're basically taxing people's pensions.

- My next major point is that if you just put that money in people's hands without them producing something that someone else wants to pay for in exchange for it, that could easily cause runaway price inflation. Just imagine everyone is suddenly given thousands of pounds. What is the first thing they will do with that money in their pockets? They go to the shops to spend it. With the rush of new customers, the shops just put their prices up to take advantage of their full wallets. Landlords, knowing their tenants have come into money, increase the rent. If the current occupants can't

---

[9] A successful friend of mine corroborated my claims. He said that since entering a higher tax bracket he found himself biased towards buying equipment for his business that he could live without because a large percentage of what he was spending would go to the government anyway if he didn't buy it. An $800 iPad would only cost him $440 taking into account what he would save in taxes by buying one. "If I wasn't being taxed at all, I'd be more fiscally conservative," he said, "It's in my interests to make my business less financially efficient by upgrading computer parts more often… After learning about all this deductions stuff, crazy priced business class flights suddenly make sense." In other words, they are aimed at people who might only be paying 55% of their face value after taking their effective tax rate into account.

pay it, there certainly will be someone else who now can.

At the moment there simply isn't enough general understanding of what money is. Money is like a token, and the value of that token is directly related to the number of goods and services in the economy. The amount of money and all the goods and services in the economy are interchangeable. That's why we spend our money on goods and services! If the amount of money in the economy increases, but the number of goods and services stays the same the money is worth less... and as the units of exchange are not generated by labour (i.e. producing more stuff) but just handed out they may even become *worthless*. In other words, one of the only reasons why money has any value at all is because it is worth the labour of others. I can use it to convince you to work for me because you can use it to convince someone else to work for you, because they can use it to convince someone else to work for someone else. It is proof the holder has served their fellow. Or at least it *should* be. Take away the labour behind it and it ceases to be a scarce and valuable commodity. People might just decide to start trading in another currency which is not just handed out freely but mostly backed by work!

- Finally, there's a subset of economics called "Public Choice Theory" which is worth looking into. *Public Choice Theory* concerns the way that economic incentives are liable to affect the behaviour of Governments, public sector bodies, and government officials – the same way that the incentives that you and I face are likely to affect our behaviour. Public Choice

Theory reveals that often governments are incentivised to give money to certain groups to get votes, or lobbying money for corporations and things like that. In most cases there will be a group that stands to benefit from handouts, but there are also groups that stand to lose. So, for example, if Starbucks thought that the government should subsidise their coffee, that might benefit Starbucks, but it would harm Costa and Nero and all their other competitors. Plus, the public would have to pay for the subsidy out of their taxes, the papers would get involved and cause a furore, so chances are it wouldn't be worth the lobbying fees for Starbucks to try and get this subsidy passed.

With the Universal Basic Income, though, it seems on the face of it there is no "out" group. Everyone at least appears to be in on the action. I fear that with the institution of a Universal Basic Income, at election time each party will seek to get elected by increasing the basic income by more than the next. It must be obvious that there is some point at which this just gets ridiculous and the basic income itself becomes untenable, otherwise we would all be millionaires already from government handouts. Unfortunately, the public will not easily be able to judge ahead of time what that breaking point is – especially with perceptions clouded by the promise of more booty! The benefits will be apparent, but the costs will be hidden up in the tax system. In reality there is only so far you can push it before it keeps chipping and chipping and chipping away at the voluntary and productive side of the economy until there is not much left to chip away from.

So, these are some of the most important arguments to consider against the Universal Basic Income. The question that is of course left is, "What else can we do?". Is there anything we can do to say make the Universal Basic Income cheaper and easier to fund? What can we do to tackle poverty and all the other problems that we want a basic income to alleviate? I want to talk about some alternative, or complementary, solutions.

Meeting Everyone's Needs

Perhaps we're starting with the wrong question. Instead of asking what we can do to alleviate poverty, perhaps we should begin with a discussion of why – after 250 years of unprecedented economic growth – we still have poverty to the degree that we have it today. Throughout all of recorded history up until the agricultural revolution, human beings lived on the equivalent of under $3 a day. It began to shoot up at the end of the 1700s and has been going up ever since. After 200 years of accelerating incomes the world average is now around $33 a day. This figure even takes into account the poor in the worst-off countries like Liberia and Afghanistan. In the most successful countries, like France, Finland and Japan, most people live on around $100 a day.[10] And look at the increase in world GDP per capita in inflation-adjusted dollars since the times of Jesus.[11]

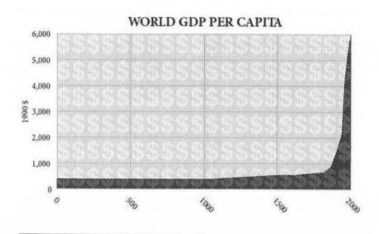

WORLD GDP PER CAPITA

---

[10] For more on these figures, and others like them, check out the great book *"Bourgeois Equality: How Ideas, Not Capital or Institutions, Enriched the World"* (2016) by economist Dr. Deirdre N. McCloskey.

[11] Ridley, M. (2010) *"The Rational Optimist"*, Fourth Estate, p11

This was achieved by advances in our modes of production. Machines were invented that allowed one person to do the work of many. In some cases, maybe hundreds. While this caused some upheaval in the short term to be sure, it also led to massive increases in the wealth and living standards of ordinary people, allowing them more leisure time to pursue their own interests. A family no longer needed to send their children to work to put food on the table for them.

Between 1870 and 1929 the average number of hours a person worked declined from 61 hours per week to 48 hours.[12] By 1970 the number had fallen to 42. That's 19 hours less, on average, in a hundred years – quite amazing![13]

As you can see from the following chart, it has continued to fall since then, but not by much. The average number of hours worked by full-time workers in the UK has remained around 37 hours since around 2001 according to figures from the UK Government (a

---

[12] McCloskey, D. N. (2016) *"Bourgeois Equality: How Ideas, Not Capital Or Institutions, Enriched the World"*, University of Chicago Press

[13] It was brought to my attention that working hours do not include commute times which may have increased. According to the 2003 *National Transport Survey* published by the Department for Transport, the average commute rose between 1972 and the mid-1990s, but fell again afterwards to 1970s levels. More recent news items claim that the average commute has risen from 48 minutes to an hour in the UK, but they do not state over what period. Employees with longer commutes get paid significantly more on average, which suggests that they are compensated for longer travel. Thanks to the widespread affordability of mobile devices with on-demand content, what may once have been "boring" commutes for many people have become opportunities to catch up on favourite podcasts and shows.

whopping 1 hour drop from the 1990s) and has fallen to 38.6 hours in America.

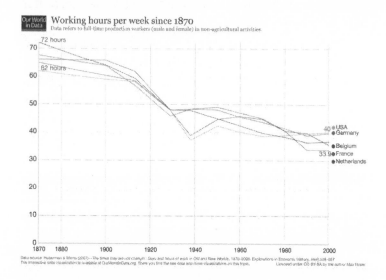

Why haven't working hours continued to decline as rapidly as they used to?

Since 1970 we have invented faster computers, information technology, internet, additional labour-saving devices. What were once expensive gadgets are now broadly affordable to people on low incomes. Things like CDs and DVDs have given way to free entertainment on YouTube and low-cost subscriptions to things like Netflix. I bought a notebook personal computer for £140, which has sound recording equipment, video editing software, two cameras, a scientific calculator, and as long as I have a web connection to Skype it could be considered a free mobile phone too. Any one of these contraptions could have set one of us back the full cost of the device itself not so long ago.

In a sense we are the most comfortable generation that has ever lived. We have everything: vacuum cleaners, dishwashers, washing machines, indoor plumbing and flush toilets, automobiles, we have machines replacing booooring factory jobs while driving down the price of the products they produce, and big combine harvesters have replaced the aching toil of farm work. You don't need millions in capital to create a massive online business, just a £300 laptop and some networking skills. Still, many people are struggling to make a living. With the huge reduction in the cost of consumer products in our lifetime and the emerging technologies of the digital age, you would think that we would have to work a lot less by now in order to earn enough to live on... and still have hoards of wealth to invest in tackling problems like poverty, homelessness, substance abuse, the epidemic of mental health issues, public health problems, and other social concerns. Surely, we could have seen yet another 19-hour reduction in the average work week since the '70s.

Perhaps we just like to buy a lot more stuff these days. We have higher expectations and want more gadgets.[14]

---

[14] It's often asserted that a single breadwinner could provide for an entire household in the 1950s, whereas now both parents usually work. In fact, a single breadwinner could still support a family today, provided they are willing to accept a 1950s standard of living. Half of people went without a telephone, washing machine, refrigerator, or central heating. Only 4% of the adult population were able to afford a TV, and only 3% a foreign holiday. We spend far less time on housework than our grandparents thanks to labour saving devices, and can expect to live at least 5 years longer.

This may certainly play a role, but if it were the primary cause then surely a far larger segment of people would be living a frugal, minimalist lifestyle in part-time employment. Most people who *did* have full time jobs would certainly feel capable of throwing money around instead of buying expensive gadgets if they chose to. Clearly the cost of living must have risen almost apace with our technological advances.[15]

Why is the cost of living so high?

I want to talk about four or five reasons. Naturally, if the cost of living is low then not only will everyone get by easier, but as a society we will have far more resources to spare to improve the condition of the needy and take them out of poverty. If I am right, that giving everyone a Universal Basic Income that would be able to pay for

---

[15] Some economists have even gone as far as to suggest that living standards and wages have been stagnating, but these claims are highly dubious. In the Washington Post article *Donald Boudreaux and Mark Perry: The Myth of a Stagnant Middle Class* (available online), the authors explain that the standard gauge of inflation underestimates the value of improvements in the quality and variety of products over time. When you compare a $500 TV from today to one from the 1970s you are not talking about the same machine. A free mp3 player on our phone has supplanted our need for a tape player. An ever-smaller percentage of people's incomes are spent on "basics" like food, shelter, clothing, and cars. The rest is spent on what they choose. The electronic products that every middle-class teenager can now afford are not much inferior to those used by the top 1% of earners. Even though the inflation-adjusted hourly wage hasn't changed much, people get far more benefits along with their wage such as pensions, paid leave, rest, and (in America) health insurance. Matt Ridley (2010) expands, "Today of Americans officially designated as 'poor' 99% have electricity, running water, flush toilets, and a refrigerator. 95% have a television, 88% a telephone, 71% a car, 70% air conditioning." Being able to afford these things is normal, whereas "the middle class of 1955, luxuriating in their cars, comforts and gadgets, would today be described as 'below the poverty line'."

all their basic needs is too expensive to be feasible at the moment, then clearly this is also necessary if we're ever going to make the basic income work. Halving the cost of living would also half the financial demands of providing everyone with a basic income.

Price Inflation

The first factor I want to discuss is price inflation. Nowadays we tend to accept that the price of everything will go up in the shops. It's a fact of life, like rain, death or taxes. But it wasn't always so. Between 1700 and 1913 the price of everything in America went down just as our phones and laptops come down in price year after year today. The U.S. did not have a single national currency until after the Civil War, but economists can still track consumer prices in terms of the exchange value of gold. In 1991, economist John J. McCusker published a historical price index of money values in the U.S., and found that the price level was actually 50% higher in 1800 than it was in 1900.[16] What happened to reverse the trend?

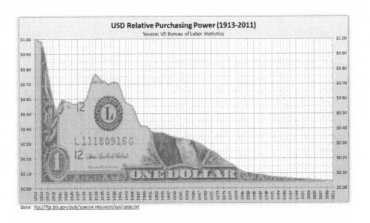

[16] McCusker, J. J. (1991) *"How Much Is That in Real Money? A Historical Price Index for Use as a Deflator of Money Values in the Economy of the United States"*, Amer Antiquarian Society.

In 1913 America instituted the Federal Reserve, their central bank, that had the authority to print money at will and lend it to The American Government at interest. Since then, the value of the dollar has gone down by 96%.

Now, we have a similar economy to America's here in the UK, and we have our own Central Bank – The Bank of England – which also has the license to print money and lend it to our government at interest. It was founded in 1694. Let's look at the damage:

Purchasing Power of the British Pound Since 1694

The degree to which the printing of money by government-licensed private banks has impeded the growth of living standards can hardly be overstated – especially for people at the bottom of the economic ladder.

The reason why is that money is a commodity as well as a means of exchange. Therefore, it is also subject to the law of supply and demand. Whenever a central bank prints more of it, the "money supply" increases, and therefore the purchasing power of the money goes down. The same wage will be able to buy less. Wages will also rise due to the inflationary effect of printing money – but not in a uniform way. The rich bankers who issue the currency will get to spend it when it has its highest value, then the initial recipients of government handouts will get it – including crony capitalists and campaign contributors. By the time regular working people get their pay rise, the price of goods will already have gone up in the shops for some time, so they will be worse off.

The printing of money is a value transfer from regular people to the politically connected. It also punishes saving and rewards debt, encouraging short-sighted behaviour and punishing people for being responsible with their income. Wealthy people who can afford to buy property to rent are major beneficiaries of this process since it devalues the large bundles of debt tied up in their mortgages while pushing up the resale price of their lets. Meanwhile, to avoid the loss of our savings to inflation, people with modest earnings have to herd huge sums of money into stock market investments and spin the wheel on them. This would not be necessary if the central banks weren't constantly printing money.

The value of money is ultimately its exchange value. If the money can buy less, then we have to work longer to pay for the things we want and need. So, I would say that the printing of money by central banks like The Federal Reserve and The Bank of England is the first cause of the major increase in the price of living. Certainly, running the presses to pay for the Universal Basic Income would be counterproductive. It doesn't take much imagination to foresee rent hikes and a speedy increase in the price of everything in the shops. If the UBI is to be instituted, it must be funded directly through taxation, and the public must insist that the central banks desist from eating away at the value of their basic income by printing money.

As to the second cause of the increase in the cost of living – what is the most expensive thing you will ever buy in your life?

...

If you said "a house" then close, but no cigar.

(Although we will be coming back to housing in just a minute...)

The Most Expensive Thing

You Will Ever Buy

In Your Life...

The actual answer is *government*. The average person in Great Britain spends between 20 and 25 years working for the government. You may draw the relevant conclusions as to how much of a drain on living standards that amounts to over the course of a lifetime. That means those people have far less to spend on goods and services that will help others find gainful employment in productive work and command a higher wage.

Granted, a large portion of the money is being spent on public services, and no doubt some will argue that the government is employing people with that cash, however, according two extensive meta-analyses[17] (combining the results from multiple studies) government services are on average twice as expensive as the same services provided by the private sector. (And this does not even account for the differences in the quality of services provided which are typically far higher in the private sector.) There are several reasons for this which I will outline extensively in a forthcoming book, *Why Governments Don't Work*, but for now a brief overview should suffice. Government departments are not in competition with other service providers, so they don't have much to compare their performance to. They can't optimise by, for example,

---

[17] T.E. Borcherding, *"The Sources of Growth in Public Expenditures in the U.S.: 1902–1970,"* in Budgets and Bureaucrats: The Sources of Government Growth, T.E. Borcherding, ed. (Durham, NC: Duke University Press, 1977), p. 62;

and J. Hilke, *"Cost Savings from Privatization: A Compilation of Study Findings,"* Reason How-To Guide #6, March 1993; J.T. Bennett and M.H. Johnson, Better Government at Half the Price (Ottawa, IL: Green Hill, 1981).

adopting best practices developed by other service providers which are constantly evolving and innovating by trying alternative approaches. They also have to be paid for out of the public purse – whether or not their services are deemed satisfactory by their users. This removes the primary incentive placed upon private companies to find ways of lowering delivery costs: pressure from customers who always want the best quality service at the best price. In fact, much of the time, even if a government department is delivering poor outcomes because it is bloated and wasteful, it can blame its poor performance on "not having enough money to do its job" and receive a bigger budget the following year. When those who receive services have a choice between service providers and can "take their business elsewhere" so to speak, it puts pressure on organisations to increase the quality of services while finding ways to decrease costs in order to keep customers happy.

According to Matt Ridley's book *The Rational Optimist* (2010),

> "As late as the mid-1800s, a stagecoach journey from Paris to Bordeaux cost the equivalent of a clerk's monthly wages; today the journey costs a day or so and is fifty times as fast. A half-gallon of milk cost the average American ten minutes of work in 1970, but only seven minutes in 1997. A three-minute phone call from New York to Los Angeles cost ninety hours of work at the average wage in

1910; today it costs less than two minutes. A kilowatt-hour of electricity cost an hour of work in 1900 and five minutes today. In the 1950s it took thirty minutes work to earn the price of a McDonald's cheeseburger; today it takes three minutes. Healthcare and education are among the few things that cost more in terms of hours worked now than they did in the 1950s."

Ridley politely abstains from mentioning what these services have in common, which is that they are two of the most state-provided. Even where private provision of education and healthcare is available, it is highly regulated to the point where only the rich can afford it. Plus, those who do avail themselves of it are paying twice. They are still taxed to fund the public schools through the tax system. If working class families could get a tax rebate to send children to a school of their choosing, this would place more of them in a position to choose a better start for their kids. (A conspiracy theorist might posit that *naturally* the elites want *some* good hospitals for themselves, and schools to send their own children to, but if a high-quality education became affordable to the masses, their position as elites could easily be usurped by the ambitious poor.)[18]

---

[18] Personally I am of the view that economic incentives are sufficient to account for most of what goes on in the world without recourse to conspiracy theories, however, there are compelling cases for some of them. I would add, though, that if there is a shadowy elite who gather in dark rooms to secretly run the world and keep people down they are doing a pretty bad job of it. World poverty is at an all-time low and continuing to decline, and people have better access to information than ever in recorded

A "moderate" (centrist) solution to this problem, which would mix the incentives for lowering costs that the market ecosystem provides with the potential for universal provision, is to have the government issue vouchers that the public can redeem for education or healthcare services at the institutions they favour. Rather than having to rely on the government to decide what they are entitled to, people could take their vouchers wherever they believed they would get the best services to meet their needs. For all its egalitarian pretensions of an equal shot for all, the present system encourages those with means to move to rich areas where the public schools and hospitals are better. The poor just have to stay put and accept whatever is doled out to them. *The Guardian* revealed that the more socially deprived an area the worse the quality and access to care on the NHS is likely to be, while *The Good Hospital Guide* demonstrated that the best performing hospitals were near the wealthiest sectors of London. The worst were in the most economically depressed areas in The East. Hospitals in rich areas had 4 times the number of doctors per hundred patients in some cases.[19]

I am not insisting that the reader take a "laissez faire" stance and adopt the hard-line position that

---

history. Perhaps they have managed to slow down the progress but they haven't managed to make it stop. For more on "rational optimism" I recommend the Steven Pinker presentation on YouTube called *Why Do Progressives Hate Progress?*

[19] DiLorenzo, T. J. (2016) *"The Problem With Socialism"*, Regnery Publishing, Ch. 9.

government should provide nothing – however – I would like to encourage a more widespread acknowledgement of the fact that if people are allowed to choose between service providers then they are likely to get a higher standard of services at a lower cost. This would result in a richer society,[20] with more money left over to spend on whatever people believe would increase their living standards. I fully appreciate that the concern of most people is whether the poor will get access to services *at all* if charges are levied for the provision of things we consider basic. Healthcare and education being primary examples. However, as things become more affordable, it also becomes easier to provide them universally.

In 1996, a laptop that cost $4699 would have a 75MHz processor and 8MB of RAM, whereas a smartphone in 2017 that costs less than $100 had a 1.5GHz processor and 2GB of RAM.[21] While clearly I use the most extreme example, reduction in the price of services in real terms is normal over time in the private sector. Rarely, if ever, does the cost of providing services go up over time. If

---

[20] Economist David B. Smith estimated in *Living With Leviathan* (2006) that if the share of government spending in the UK had remained constant since 1960, then national output by 2005 would have at least doubled. It's hard to imagine that the poor would not be far better off in absolute terms under those conditions than they are now.

[21] It's worth mentioning that in a sane society the price of healthcare provision should go down every year, not just because of technological innovation, but because people were living healthier lives and getting less sick. Our current modes of provision do not incentivise this because the only thing remunerated within the system is poor health. It is really a system of "sick care" rather than "health care". For more details stay tuned for my forthcoming book *Why Is Healthcare So Expensive in America?*

we could see even a percentage of the same effect in education and healthcare (as well as property development which we are about to come to) it would be easy to meet the costs of universal provision.

Fortunately, real-world examples of what I describe are beginning to emerge despite the present constraints of our system. *ReasonTV* reported that an American entrepreneur was recently able to create a network of cheap private schools in North Carolina and educate each child for around $5,500 – as compared to the state which was paying about $9,300 per student to offer an inferior quality of education.[22] Since I released the first edition of this book on kindle, a similar scheme has emerged in England. Award-winning British researcher James Tooley, who wrote a book called *The Beautiful Tree*, on how poor people across the world manage to educate themselves, had begun a project to open a chain of low-cost private schools charging only £2,700 a year. This is way below average private school fees of £17,000 and something like half what the government spends on average per student in state schools.[23]

In health care, MD, Dr. Keith Smith, opened a Surgery Centre in Oklahoma that provided services so cheaply that other hospitals had to respond by lowering their own tariffs – creating a deflationary effect, not only in Oklahoma but even in further flung places.[24] One

---

[22] "A Libertarian Builds Low-Cost Private Schools for the Masses" available on YouTube: https://www.youtube.com/watch?v=gOJiayZoNDI
[23] Weale, S. (2018) *"Low-cost, no-frills Durham private school attacked by teachers"* The Guardian, retrieved online.
[24] Sammeroff, A. (2017) *"What Libertarianism Can Do For The Poor."*

patient, upon finding their website, made a print-out quoting the cost of a prostate operation at $3,600 and took it into his local hospital in Georgia who were ready to charge him $40,000 for the same procedure. When he phoned Dr. Smith apologetically to report that they had offered to price-match the combined cost of the surgery and his air fares to Oklahoma (saving him $36,000) Keith said the story itself would prove far more valuable than the $3,600 he would have charged.[25]

This kind of innovation is desperately needed here to make limited resources stretch further and do more good. Unfortunately, as it stands, we are seeing the opposite effect in action. Despite the budget of the National Health Service in the UK doubling in real terms between 1995 and 2015 according to *The Institute for Fiscal Studies*, the number of people languishing on government waiting lists is set to rise from 4.4 million to 5 million by 2021 according to *The Guardian*, a left-leaning paper that is very much in favour of our NHS.[26] How often is the government forking out tens of thousands for procedures that could be done at a tenth of the cost by someone like Dr. Keith Smith?

Another "moderate" solution (which will no doubt still

Scottish Libertarian Party. Retrieved online: http://scottishlibertarians.com/poverty/.

[25] Graboyes, R. F. (2016) *"Transparent Health Care Pricing — Keith Smith and the Surgery Center of Oklahoma"* InsideSources, retrieved online.

[26] Campbell, D. (2017) *"Hospital waiting lists 'will rise above 5 million' as targets slide."* The Guardian, retrieved online.

smack of controversy) would be to reserve 'free' public healthcare and schooling for those who cannot afford to pay for it. Those with the means to pay could be charged a percentage of total costs in proportion to their income and ability to pay in order to ensure there are enough resources to ensure universality of services. They could pay their costs back out of their wages over a period rather than in a lump sum, so the mechanism would emulate a regular (pay as you earn) tax for public services. Many more people would opt then to get private insurance and schooling rather than pay fees out of their wages, and this would unburden the taxpayer from providing services to the wealthy. Public funds would be saved for those who really need them. I'm not for this policy per se, because it sounds like it would be complicated and costly to administrate – plus it might actually turn into a "poverty trap" of its own, where people don't want to earn more in case they have to fork out more for their healthcare and education. I mention it, though, as one possible option worthy of consideration.

Certainly, if a universal basic income is on the cards then the government will probably have to find ways to cut spending to pay for it. If we trust people enough to put money in their hands, we should also hand them the right to choose who provides their most basic services rather than have the government decide what they are entitled to and from whom.

Now, to return to the topic of housing.

House Prices

When I asked the audience whom I initially made this presentation to, how much they thought house prices had increased between 1971 and 2011 the first guess was 300%. The next was 500%... there was a palpable gasp when I revealed the figure reported by the charity *Shelter*, which was four thousand, two hundred and fifty five percent (4255%).[27] Someone exclaimed, appalled, that I must be kidding – to which I replied "I'm not f**king kidding you," receiving a sympathetic laugh.

The Telegraph reported that according to the charity Shelter, the typical value of a house had increased by just over 43 times since 1971, from £5,632 to £245,319.[28] According to the same source, if a family's weekly shop had increased at the same rate, it would now stand at £453, which is six times the actual figure of around £75. In 1981 the average homebuyer in The States was between the ages of 25 and 34. In 2017 the typical homebuyer was 44.[29] Over 50% of young people in the UK believe they will never own a house, while people in this country once used to be able to budget

---

[27] Ahead of writing the foreword to the book, Bob Murphy expressed understandable scepticism towards this figure, saying he thought I must be "f--king kidding" too. Doing due diligence he checked it against *The Halifax House Price Index*, the UK's longest running monthly house price series with data covering the whole country. Although they only have figures dating back to 1983, they produce a far more modest figure. According to them we are only paying between 6 and 7 times as much for our homes as people were in 1983. I have kept the original figure cited in my talk included for colour as even if this is greatly exaggerated the following points and policy prescriptions still stand. You can find *The Halifax House Price Index* online.

[28] Oxlade, A. (2013) *"How house prices have risen 43-fold since 1971"*, *The Telegraph*, retrieved online.

[29] Bloom, E. (2017)*"Here's the surprising truth about first-time home buyers"* CNBC, retrieved online.

for a house with only one bread winner. Why are house prices so expensive?

This, too, can largely be explained by *Public Choice Theory*. At any one time there is a 9:1 ratio of people who own houses to people who are looking to buy. What we have here is a *group-rationality failure.*[30]

---

[30] *Group-rationality failure* is a useful term coined by economics writer and editor Sheldon Richman. It applies to any scenario where the rational course of action for any individual member of a group is at odds with what is rational for the group to do as a whole. The most famous example in economics is called "the problem of the commons." It describes a situation where land is held in common by a number of grazers. In the long run, it's in everyone's interest to farm sustainably so the land can be used indefinitely. However, since the land is held in common, it is in the short-term interest of each individual grazer to feed their livestock as much as possible – especially considering the fact that if they don't then others still

While it stands to benefit each of us to pay as little as possible for our own house, it's not in anyone's interest to have to default on their mortgage because the value of the house they are already living in has plummeted... even if they might turn out the better for it in the long term. With far more people owning a house than looking for one at any one time, letting house prices fall is never going to be much of a vote winner.[31]

Under the Conservative Government of the UK in the early 1990s, prime minister John Major presided over a fall in house prices and the public reacted badly. The collapse of property prices between 1989 and 1994 made them unelectable.[32] The golden rule was thus established for all future administrations: *Thou Shalt Not Let House Prices Fall*. Ever since, successive governments have been finding all sorts of ways they claim are "in the public interest" to keep house prices

---

probably will. If everyone does what is rational for them personally, the commonly-held land will soon be depleted. So what is rational for the individual is not rational for the group. They will have to come up with some kind of agreement to "solve" the problem of the commons. Some people think the government will have to step in and regulate the commons, others say the best solution is to privatise the land giving each a portion so they all have the incentive to maintain their own section. It's worth noting that it's in the interests of each individual to pay as little tax as possible while extracting as much value as they can from the government in the form of public services and handouts, but if everyone did that successfully then the state would go bankrupt leaving no public services for anyone. Therefore, we could conclude, that government itself is susceptible to the problem of the commons.

[31] It would also mean the government would have to accept less in property taxes, which provides an additional disincentive since they'd have to find other ways to make up the revenue which might make them unpopular.

[32] Frisby, D. (2016) *"Why younger people can't afford a house: money became too cheap"*, The Guardian. Retrieved online.

up. Only a few large companies are allowed to build any houses in the UK, and far less than are necessary to meet the rise in demand. Copious regulations and restrictions on land use and buildings, planning and zoning laws, building codes, height restrictions even outside of the city centre. All of these restrict the supply of available housing and push house prices and rents up. Landlord registration, stamp duty, *House in Multiple Occupation* (HMO) licensing in Scotland – which has left so many apartments under-occupied while other people can't afford housing by disallowing more than two people from renting together if they are not related. All of these increase the demand for housing and push up the cost of buying or renting.

In the UK, building on so-called "greenbelt" land surrounding cities is prohibited (and politically opposed) in part because of the emotive misnomer they have been given. Many assume these are rich environmental heritage sites, when in fact most of them are anything but. They are not lands which are particularly valuable from an environmental perspective or as amenities, but agricultural land, very unattractive to look at, mostly inaccessible to the public, much of it not even commercially viable as farming land if not for agricultural subsidies, and largely prime real estate in areas with very high housing demand. This land is prohibited from being used for what it is desired for, which is to give people affordable places to live.[33]

---

[33] People hold genuine concerns about unsightly housing estates springing up in their "backyards", but housing developments need not be

Besides this, interest rates have been priced far below their market rate for 50 years or more by the central banks, turning property into a lucrative investment rather than something people buy simply to live in. This must have been especially fruitful for those already wealthy enough to make down payments on several properties in order to let them, but not particularly fortunate for those not yet on the property ladder! As rates have been kept near zero for many years, sometimes even dipping below, more buyers have been galvanised to take out mortgages and enter the market for real estate, and so house prices have unsurprisingly increased. Add to this the money printing which I mentioned earlier which also has an inflationary effect on the price of accommodation, and even help-to-buy schemes which sound benign but drive more money into the housing market than would otherwise be there.[34]

---

unattractive. There must be any number of ingenious architects that would relish the opportunity to design beautiful complexes for people to live in. Unfortunately, under the current pressures to turn a profit in a system where prices are inflated and tenants are scrambling for the most affordable accommodation that they can lay their hands on, aesthetics will usually be the first thing to go. Landlords are not under pressure to provide attractive buildings under the current climate. As my friend Richard Cox put it in his interview with me on *The Deep State Consciousness* podcast, the seen ugliness is that of the new, cheap apartment complexes – the unseen ugliness is people slogging away for longer hours in jobs they hate rather than spending time with their families because the house prices are so high.

[34] To exemplify, imagine you are a used-car salesman. Naturally, you try to sell each of your vehicles for the best price you can fetch for them. Then one day the government declares that used cars are a human right, and that everyone should be able to afford one. They offer to put a 25% subsidy towards every used car purchase from now on. Would you not just raise your prices by 25%? This is roughly what is happening in the housing market. The one safeguard against you doing this would be other car dealers only raising their prices by 24%, and then 23%, and so on. The

Clearly, there are no perfect solutions on meeting the spiralling demand for housing, only trade-offs. Either we build out, or we build up, or allow more people to live in smaller spaces, or we halt immigration, or we accept that a larger and larger percentage of our incomes will be spent on having somewhere to live.

For our American readers the picture is not much different. Here is a graph showing median family income as compared to median price of housing in the states.[35]

---

supply of housing is so limited that there is little mitigating effect from competition between alternative suppliers.

[35] Saunders, P. (2018) *"Quobands: A Funding Mechanism for Crowd Construction"* hosted by SSRN, retrieved online: https://papers.ssrn.com/sol3/papers.cfm?abstract_id=3107645.

In the interests of rigour, I should note that there may be a problem with using these figures as evidence. Since the value shown is only median housing values, it says nothing about the quality or size of the housing. The houses might, on average, be much nicer, better designed and much bigger. The average house may be providing greater utility than in the past.* Something important for the young economist to always bear in mind when making comparisons is: Are you comparing apples to apples? *For example, a TV today is a completely different machine to one you might have bought in the 1950s. You may be paying the same price for a machine and still be getting a far better piece of equipment. Comparing average prices alone will not tell you one way or another.*

* After first publishing the above remarks, my suspicions were confirmed when I stumbled upon a 2014 article by Mark J. Perry (published online by the American Enterprise Institute) reporting that in the U.S. "new homes are 1,000 square feet larger than in 1973, and the living space per person has doubled over last 40 years.".

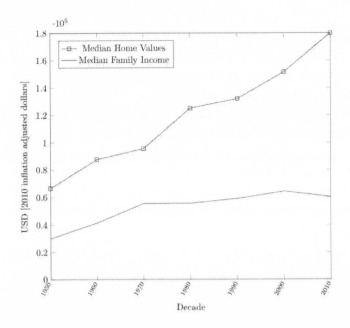

A report on the YouTube channel *ReasonTV* covered the story of an LA Musician who built "tiny" solar-powered houses for the homeless at the cost of $1,200 each. He crowdfunded $100,000 to kick-off the grass-roots project aimed at helping the needy and alleviating poverty, only to find police and garbage crews descending upon the homes – ordered by the city to seize and destroy them.[36]

Meanwhile, a media outlet dedicated to driving sustainability reported upon a Russian company that was able to 3D print a tiny house in 24 hours at the

---

[36] ReasonTV (2016) *"This LA Musician Built $1,200 Tiny Houses for the Homeless. Then the City Seized Them."*, retrieved online on YouTube.

coldest time of the year. The whole house cost only $10,134.[37] Even using conventional methods, a two-bedroom timber-frame house can be put up for around costs £25,000. Since houses aren't exactly expensive to *build*, we can draw the necessary conclusion that the reason why they are expensive to *buy* is the excess of regulation.

Now, we might stand from a distance and argue that the government indeed *should* place restrictions upon who can rent to whom and in which circumstances. For example, to make sure apartments don't get overcrowded, or intervene to ensure that certain minimum standards are in place to prevent "slum landlords" from taking advantage of their tenants. However, we should hold no illusion as to where the costs of complying with these regulations will come from. They will hardly be coming out of the landlord's pockets on a seller's market. Occupants will be forced to fork out higher rents to cover the additional fees. With so many people scrambling for what limited accommodation there is, the landlord can always rent to the highest bidder. The best defence against "slum landlords" is not more government regulations but allowing lots of places to be built so that the supply of accommodation is more than ample. Where housing is scarce people have to take what they can get, but if it is plentiful then landlords have to compete to attract

[37] Alter, L. (2017)*"Russian company 3D prints a tiny house in 24 hours"*, Treehugger, retrieved online: https://www.treehugger.com/tiny-houses/russian-company-3d-prints-tiny-house-24-hours.html

tenants by offering the best place at the best price.

Some people might want to save money on rent, for example, by accepting crowded conditions in the short term so that they can buy their own house sooner rather than later. Personally, I do not think the government has any business standing in the way of what they deem to be in their interest. Supposing a group of students wanted to convert their living room into an extra bedroom and sublet it to keep their outgoings low. Yes, it might be crowded for a while, but far less so than many people have lived throughout the vast majority of civilisation where large families lived in tiny houses. Supposing the occupants have part time jobs as well as studying. They do their fair share of partying too, and spend long stints doing homework in the library between classes. They are not likely to be home that much and may just want to use their apartment as somewhere to sleep. It seems a waste for them to rack up additional student debt to pay disproportionately for digs that far exceed their actual needs. If the nanny state will allow people to make the choices they want, it will free up spaces and lead to lower rental fees for everyone.

A free market would increase the supply of accommodation and reduce the cost of renting, while putting a natural pressure on landlords to maintain their properties to a higher standard in order to attract tenants from the bottom-up without many (or any) top-down regulations from the government. The widespread availability of places to stay would regulate the landlords and force them to maintain their property and invest in safety equipment.

Government regulations attempt to ensure acceptable standards, but in reality they only enforce one-size-fits-all solutions which lack nuance and flexibility. They are fated to forever miss the mark when it comes to meeting the preferences of real people, because doing so across an entire economy is frankly an impossible task. People's needs differ radically from area to area, property to property, and even individual to individual. Perfection exists only in the conceptual mind, not in reality. We would all love a place that is cheap, big, well-located, near shops and amenities, gets the sun in summer, and has every other conceivable virtue a house might have. But everyone has different priorities. Some people will prefer a quiet place, some prefer somewhere close to the action. Someone might prize a place nearer their work, while others enjoy listening to podcasts on the commute and would sooner take a further place that has nice cafés and bars nearby. Some people would rather pay more for their own space – their idea of heaven is a house with extra rooms. Others would sooner get a crowded place with plenty of friends to chat to. Landlords have the feedback mechanism of profit and loss to let them know what the needs of people in their area are. If other buildings in the area are soundproofed but theirs is not, then they may have to accept less in rent money, or take on less dependable tenants if that is something people find desirable in their area. The same principle applies to all tenant preferences. Landlords will soon be made aware of what people want when they show up for viewings. Sellers on a free market simply have access to local information which regulators in government do not. They also have skin in the game. If they don't meet a sufficient amount of preferences, they themselves stand to lose out on a profit. Bottom line is, we should trust people to make the best trade-offs for themselves. A government policy-maker can't possibly know what tenants would most like their landlords to invest in because it varies so widely from person to person and place to place. To mandate blindly across the board is often to force wasteful spending on things that many people don't even want or need.

Final word on housing. Putting aside the figure of four thousand and something percent that house prices may have risen between 1971 and 2011 in the UK. Just imagine that buying or renting a home cost a quarter of what it does now… or even just a half of what it does now... How much wealthier would we be?... How much less costly would it be to house the homeless, and provide for the basic needs of everyone with the additional resources we would have to spare?

It is not abnormal for people to spend 30% of their income maintaining a roof over their head. Significantly reducing that figure would be a beneficial end in itself, but it would also perhaps be a necessary preliminary to instituting a Universal Basic Income that was in any way sustainable or affordable. Without easing government restrictions on the supply of housing we might expect rent hikes to follow as a direct result of the UBI, which will only privilege wealthy proprietors who already benefit disproportionately from the current economy.

Cheaper Stuff

Most people tend to think of business regulations as an unambiguous good, but they are not without their own trade-offs. Businesses in the UK currently spend £80 billion a year complying with regulations[38] – or £1200 for each man, woman and child in Great Britain. Much of these costs are passed onto customers in the form of higher prices. Some of them come out of potential staff earnings, and the rest come out of company profits. Profits might otherwise be reinvested in growing these businesses or spent by shareholders on goods and services that would put people into productive work. Unnecessary regulations also create lots of busy work for bureaucrats, accountants, actuaries, auditors, lawyers, administrators and regulators who all have to be paid to go through forms rather than to produce something that improves living standards in a tangible way. This is not to mention that countless practitioners, professionals and small business owners now have to spend endless hours filling out forms instead of doing what they are trained to do, which is to serve their customers. Were these people free to invest more of their time using their talents creatively to serve their customers there would be more wealth to go around. Everything would be cheaper. Instead they are forced to spend countless hours pushing papers and keeping filing cabinets full of records, most of which will never be looked at again.

More people would start businesses if the legal demands weren't so intimidating. Bakers want to bake

[38] Gammell, K. (2010) *"Regulation costs UK businesses £80bn a year"*, The Telegraph, retrieved online.

cakes. Computer programmers want to code. Photographers want to take snaps. No one goes into business thinking, "Gee, I can't wait to spend half my time filling out government forms! Between that and managing my staff I'll barely have any time to use my skills to work with customers which is what I started my own company to do the first place."

People assume that without reams of regulatory codes people will freely sell snake oil and defective products, but actually our common law courts are adequately equipped to deter companies from false advertising or selling faulty products already. These are prosecutable offences. Many of our Kafkaesque legislative codes are completely unnecessary, however, politicians need to be seen to be doing something, so they write regulations into law.

Typically, over-regulating favours the big players who can afford the additional legal personnel, accountants, actuaries, and other staff to comply with the rules – or find ways around them. Small businesses find it hard to bear the financial burden. It will take up a much larger percentage of their time and resources. "Deregulation" is the scare word, but ironically large companies often lobby the government for *more* regulations rather less in order to reduce competition from upstarts. In fact, according to *The Sunlight Foundation*, (a non-partisan, non-profit organization that aims to make government more accountable and transparent,) for each of the 5.8 billion dollars spent by America's 200 most politically active corporations between 2007 and 2012 on federal lobbying and campaign contributions they got $741 in return in kickbacks and benefits.[39] This poses a tremendous threat to the integrity of our institutions, because as soon as it becomes more profitable for a business to lobby the government than to serve their customers then that is what they will do. Lobbying will become their first priority. This is why government is often a corrupting actor in the economy rather than a referee. The mutual benefit to politicians and big business interests of getting in bed together will often outweigh the benefits of serving the public.[40] Economists call this *Regulatory Capture*.

Cutting unnecessary red-tape severs the link, frees up the cost of compliance and brings down prices. It frees up man hours for creating things that actually improve people's living standards rather than lobbying and filling out forms. It also evens the playing field between small businesses and large corporations.

In my article *Beauty Salon Economics,* I explained that the economy is not just like a chess board where you can move one piece with deterministic and predictable consequences, but an intricate fabric where any one move can create a cascade of domino effects. I illustrate with an example:

> "Supposing some of the fancy hair
> salons are getting irked because cheap

[39] Allison, B. and Harkins, S. (2014) *"Fixed Fortunes: Biggest corporate political interests spend billions, get trillions"*, retrieved online: https://sunlightfoundation.com/2014/11/17/fixed-fortunes-biggest-corporate-political-interests-spend-billions-get-trillions/

[40] I found a cool video on YouTube that brilliantly illustrates this point called *Capitalism and The State*, access it here: https://www.youtube.com/watch?v=x3drasEFZNk

salons are popping up everywhere and giving people poor quality haircuts. They're giving the whole industry a bad name. So, a coalition goes to the government to pass standards and licensing laws in the hairdressing industry (in some places you currently need a license to braid hair.) That's going to improve the quality of haircuts going around, right?

Not necessarily. Now all the hair salons have to send their employees to college for two years to get a license, and when they graduate they are expecting much higher pay because they just sunk two years into an education during which they didn't see any money. Some of them went out drinking with their student loans, the rest still had rent to pay, and most of them accumulated debts. What's more the salons need to consult special accountants or lawyers to make sure they can prove that they are adhering to the new regulations — even the ones who are way ahead of the law and already providing far better conditions and services than what has been mandated. These professionals often charge upwards of $100 an hour. Many independent salons simply can't afford the increase in costs and have to close down entirely; others have to jack prices up to pay for the extra costs of compliance and staff. In some areas only one salon is left standing and since people have less choice they can afford to let standards slip.

With the price of haircuts going up lots of people decide to go without. They cut their friends' hair at home, badly. Or they get pretty good at it and don't have to go to the hairdressers anymore but take longer to prepare for going out and miss out on the chat and gossip. What's more, everyone who does still go for a professional haircut has less left over to spend on a manicure or something else nice, so other industries also suffer. You can add to that the marginal increase in taxes to pay the civil servants in the new public body which acts as a regulator for the hairdressing industry. Now those people are involved in busy work instead of making commodities and providing services that improve people's living standards in real terms and rather than paying into the public purse they are a net drain on it."[41]

My article goes on to provide an alternative to government oversight of the beauty industry:

---

[41] Read it here: www.therationalrise.com/beauty-salon-economics/

"A series of private watchdogs to certify only hairdressers that meet their standards and give the ones who do an official number and sticker to put in their window; because [the watchdogs] are competing they have to keep the costs of certification to a minimum (no $100 an hour fees), and people who are not fussed to pay extra for a certified cut can take a risk on somewhere cheaper or go by word of mouth."[42]

Don't look now, but there are over 800 occupations that might require a licence in some states in America including a tour guide, manicurist, dog walker, librarian, locksmith, dry cleaner, auctioneer, fruit ripener, plumber, private investigator, Christmas tree vendor, florist, interior designer, funeral director, cab driver, shampoo specialist, glass installer, cat groomer, tree groomer, hunting guide, kick boxer, real estate agent, tattoo artist, nutritionist, acupuncturist, music therapist, yoga instructor and mortician.

Occupational licensing makes for an interesting case because it is almost ubiquitously considered in the public interest and even necessary to prevent catastrophe, and yet there is actually zero evidence that it leads to a higher quality of service provision. Zilch!

---

[42] For more on how the free market could regulate private businesses it's worth reading my article called *Occupational Licensing*, www.therationalrise.com/occupational-licensing/. It provides a comprehensive list.

On the contrary, after compiling a meta-analysis entitled, *Rule of Experts*, S. David Young had to conclude that "most of the evidence suggests that licensing has, at best, a neutral effect on quality and may even cause harm to the consumers... The higher entry standards imposed by licensing laws reduce the supply of professional services.... The poor are net losers because the availability of low-cost service has been reduced." Stanley Gross of Indiana State University, had to concur stating that, "mainly the research refutes the claim that licensing protects the public." The most recent analyses I could find are by economics PhD. Morris Kleiner, who released two publications (2006, 2013) for the Upjohn Institute for Employment Research, demonstrating that licensing occupations does more to restrict competition than to ensure quality.

The Obama administration found the same, when in 2015 the President sent his council of economic advisers out on a fact-finding mission to discover why job creation was so hard for the administration. The council – made up of Democrats, not ideological free marketeers – concluded that demands for mandatory occupational licensing were creating terrible cartels, excluding workers and getting in the way of regular people wanting to start up businesses.[43]

---

[43] Furman, J. and Giuliano, L. (2015) *"New Data Show that Roughly One-Quarter of U.S. Workers Hold an Occupational License"*, The WHITE HOUSE of President Obama, official site archives. Retrieved online: https://obamawhitehouse.archives.gov/blog/2016/06/17/new-data-show-roughly-one-quarter-us-workers-hold-occupational-license

Universal Basic Income advocates want people to take out their government money and retrain themselves or start new companies. If they do, they may soon be confronted with the reality of how hard it is to navigate through all the rules and codes they are supposed to comply with in order to do so. Countless people have already reported being so confounded by the difficulties of hiring and firing that they choose not to bother, running their small businesses on their own instead of expanding. Ambitious individuals, often from poor backgrounds, are expected to hire expensive staff or go out and get costly licenses before they even start working. They used to be able to just turn up as apprentices and get training on the job. All these things will create impediments to regular people advancing themselves in the new economy and creating wealth. They also increase the potential cost of providing a Basic Income.

It's time to cut the red tape. Not for the sake of the rich, but for the sake of the poor.

Free Trade

Before we go on to some questions, I want to finish with a few words on free trade.

We are currently prohibited by our governments from importing many goods from some of the poorest countries in the world. In cases where we *are* permitted, the imported goods are often taxed heavily.[44] This hurts the poor, both at home and abroad. Those in poorer nations are harmed because they aren't allowed to sell their produce to us, bringing in precious currency to invest in infrastructure, schooling, healthcare, fuel, power, communications technology, transportation, and everything else they need to become developed, wealthy and self-sufficient. The few big companies who *are* allowed to operate in these countries can pay knock-down wages because they don't face much competition from other employers who would bid-up the price of labour and improve working conditions given the chance. This impedes the flow of capital investment into developing countries which would generate wealth, machines, factories, technology, infrastructure, training, skills and expertise to destitute populations who desperately need them to escape a subsistence lifestyle. Meanwhile, we are forced to pay more for goods that we could import more cheaply from abroad. Instead we have to produce them within our borders, or import them from other rich countries with similar economies to our own. We have less left over in our pockets and must admit lower standards of living. This particularly harms the least

---

[44] The fact we even need the permission of our wise overlords to import something from abroad smacks of intrusion.

well off, who spend the largest percentage of their income on basic essentials.

Clearly, this situation is not only injurious but inhumane. So why does it continue?

Economist Bryan Caplan shone a light on some plausible explanations in his book (and YouTube presentations) entitled *The Myth of the Rational Voter* (2007). Caplan elucidated the findings of a study called the *Survey of Americans and Economists on the Economy* (1996). The survey demonstrated that the views of the general public seem to differ in very particular, *systematic* ways from the views popularly held within the economics profession. While people who study economics may disagree in many ways, and on many issues, they tend to share some particular understandings which give them an edge over the general public in demystifying the world. Lay people lean towards specific prejudices which make them susceptible to reaching flawed conclusions on economic issues. Politicians then have to cater to their misapprehensions to have any hope of being elected.[45]

One of these misapprehensions is that the public tend to underestimate the social benefits of markets. Lay people are suspicious of people making profits from solving problems, whereas economists tend to think that if a profit is to be made from solving a problem

---

[45] I ask you to recall what I mentioned earlier about having come to see that economics is not so much about the immediate and apparent effects of any policy, but the knock-on effects which will not necessarily be intuitively predictable.

then it won't be long before a workable solution is found. People are likely to take an interest in solving it when there is money to gain. Economists are far more worried about problems which are hard to imagine someone making a profit from solving. Air pollution, for example.

The public also tend to have heightened pessimism about the future of the economy over those in the economic profession. Most people see things going badly, whereas economists think of things bouncing up and down but largely across an upward trend over the long-term.

A third prejudice is a species of anti-foreign bias that causes the public to anticipate more negative outcomes from globalisation, foreign trade, cooperation, and immigration. They are more likely than economists are to think that there is something radically different between trading with someone who lives abroad as compared to someone who lives in their own country. They are more likely to believe that problematic outcomes will arise domestically from buying products from abroad. This is an intuitive misgiving which many people hold due to what economists have termed *concentrated benefits and dispersed costs*. The concept has immense explanatory power when it comes to understanding why many policies are popular (or unpopular) and what the likely effects of those policies may be. The idea is that a policy can be conspicuously beneficial to small group of people, while its costs are inconspicuously spread amongst such a large group of people (perhaps *everyone* else) as to be veiled into obscurity.[46] Subsidies to sugar and tobacco farmers in America are often cited as an example. Why would the government continue to give handouts to producers of products that are known to be harmful? It's because the benefits to the recipients are concentrated, while the costs to the taxpayer are spread so thinly that most people don't even notice they are paying them.

To illustrate the point in the context of free trade, if a factory making curtains in Britain closes down due to competition from one in Morocco, it's easy to see the 60 unemployed factory workers, and a local newspaper will likely write an article decrying the government for allowing cheap imports. What passes unseen, though, is that everyone in the UK who buys curtains now has some extra cash left over to spend on things that will put other people into work. There is a net benefit.

Perhaps as a consequence of these popular misconceptions, free trade has never been very popular on either side of the political spectrum. The right tend to believe that people in poorer countries are "taking our jobs"; while the left believe that by helping other countries sell their exports and industrialise we are "exploiting them". One only need understand the Classical Economist David Ricardo's theory of *comparative advantage* to see that both criticisms are deeply flawed. In short, Ricardo explained that every person and nation is better suited to certain forms of

---

[46] I refer the reader once more to Bastiat's essay *That Which is Seen and That Which is Not Seen* for a fuller exploration of the phenomenon, retrievable online: http://bastiat.org/en/twisatwins.html.

production than others, and when each specialises in what they are good at, overall production is greater, and everyone ends up better off for it. Each time we trade we are better off. If I swap you a tie for a pencil in a voluntary exchange, then clearly you prefer the tie and I prefer the pencil. We have each gained without creating anything new. The more we trade the more everyone gets of what they want. The more well off we all become. Exploitation happens in the largest part when people's trade options are limited so they have to take whatever they can get. When people have a multiplicity of options to choose from, they tend to pick the best deal for themselves and can improve their situation over time.[47]

On that note, let's talk about the real history of neo-colonialism. Its cruel effects have often been blamed on free trade when a cursory glance at the evidence will soon reveal that they were caused by anything but.

In the 1970s, when the price of oil increased, the Middle Eastern countries who sold it invested their new found wealth in Western Banks, which in turn invested their money in the third world. This was regarded as a sound venture as countries don't tend to disappear or go under with the regularity of unsuccessful corporations. Unfortunately, most of the money was

---

[47] A good analogy for global free trade would be shopping for second-hand books online. Buyers match up with people who are trying to sell what they are looking for, and can shop around for the best price even on rare books. Sellers get access to buyers they would not have found very easily before. It's true that some second-hand book stores may have lost out or had to adjust, but the majority of people are richer for the option of buying online, and more books find a happy home.

lent to military governments and tyrants who had no intentions of spending it on the welfare of their people, and those people are now suffering from a burden of debt which they didn't even create. Pan-national financial authorities like the International Monetary Fund, The World Trade Organisation and The World Bank insisted that these countries increase exports to pay off these loans in exchange for additional relief, but these shakedowns would often create a glut in the market for the exported products, pushing prices through the floor so that little additional income was even earned by their sale. In 1996, Africa had amassed more than $400 billion dollars of foreign debt, and 40 cents out of every dollar they earned on exports had to be spent to service that debt, leaving little left over for them to import essentials from abroad.[48]

The money that African and South American nations gained from selling their rich natural resources to Western countries was, for a long time, spent largely on manufactured goods from Europe and North America. This was because our governments imposed trade barriers to prevent their people from buying cheaper manufactured goods from abroad where labour costs were still low.[49] One could argue, cynically, that these

---

[48] Ayittey, B. N. (1997) *"Africa in Chaos"*, Macmillan Press Ltd., p31.

[49] I say *still* low because if we had opened free trade instead, lots of companies would rush into the poorest areas in the world to take advantage of low wages and bring development and investment with them. Wages would begin to rise and local ancillary firms would crop up to serve the international producers. Even if some of those companies had to relocate after a time to take advantage of less expensive labour elsewhere, they would be sending money to where it was most needed and leaving the economy in a better shape than they found it. Afterwards there would be

policies were implemented deliberately *to keep poor places poor for as long as possible so that rich corporations could import cheap natural resources from them, rather than face competition from foreign manufacturers taking advantage of low labour costs at home*.

The political left, who were (to their credit) the major critics of these "neo-liberal" policies, diagnosed the problem but misdiagnosed the cause due to their ideological commitment to opposing capitalism. They blamed markets themselves, when in reality it was intervention into the function of markets by governments and international financial institutions which caused these abuses and stunted the economic growth of developing nations for decades. The stultification continues.

European Nations *have* done a great deal of damage to some places in the developing world through colonialism, propping up dictators, and expropriating natural resources. Many economists, both on the left and the right, have even argued that dumping our own unwanted surplus food produce on a large scale in developing countries has had the effect of putting local producers out of business and stopping them from growing their own domestic economies. (Others dispute that giving a nation free produce can ever logically make them poorer.) Our leaders have given aid

---

considerably more wealth in circulation for people to invest in local ventures as well as new infrastructure, factories, machines. They would also have more skills and expertise behind them.

in the form of arms to dictatorial governments and helped them oppress their people.[50] Other times, they have stipulated that a high percentage of aid given to poor countries be spent on goods produced here that weren't wanted or needed by them,[51] handing out corporate welfare to cronies and campaign contributors in big business at home out of the public purse. Western nations have indeed pursued any number of policies that may have harmed developing nations.[52] But one way we have not harmed them is through free trade. In fact, now we are harming them by forbidding free trade.

I believe if we had been completely open to international exchange decades ago we may have ended world poverty by today – but sadly mine remains the minority position. The right still think foreigners will take our jobs. President Trump campaigned on a platform of protectionism.[53] And the left still think we

---

[50] In a particularly egregious case, the government of France backed the Hutu government of Juvénal Habyarimana in the massacre of nearly a million Tutsis.

[51] For an example of these antics, in 1986 the British Government strong-armed the government of India into accepting aid in the form of 21 Westland Helicopters that they didn't particularly want or need by stating that they were unlikely to receive the aid in any other form. The cost of just one of those helicopters represented the cost of the entire development program for Ethiopia and this was far from an isolated incident.

[52] For a fuller exploration of the specific ways that Western meddling "compounded Africa's crisis" in the post-colonial period, I refer the reader to Chapter 8 of Ghanaian economist George Ayittey's truly excellent book *Africa in Chaos* (1998).

[53] *Protectionism* is the term given by economists to the practice of taxing imports in the hope of shielding a country's domestic industries from foreign competition. The case for protectionism was thought to have been put to bed by the Liberal Classical Economists such as Adam Smith and David Ricardo, however, the sophisms of the protectionists seem ever-

are exploiting people by offering to exchange our money for their produce. They repeat seductive but vacuous slogans like *"fair trade not free trade"*, without ever defining what a fair trade would look like, or acknowledging that free trade is certainly not what we have had so far. What's more, they intend to impose their ideas of who should be allowed to trade with whom and under what circumstance, by force, upon the people of Planet Earth – in an authoritarian fashion – whether they like it or not.

Throughout most of the neo-liberal period (beginning around 1980 and persisting until today) there was indeed much extreme poverty in the world, and people blamed this on the new appetite for capitalism expressed by leaders like Margaret Thatcher and Ronald Reagan. These were politicians who preached the virtues of limited government while vastly increasing the size of the states which they presided over. "Fiscally Conservative" Ronald Reagan more than tripled the Gross Federal Debt from $900 billion to over $2.7 trillion, an increase of more than his eight predecessors combined.[54] All the problems of this period were largely blamed on "free markets", even though most of these problems were inherited from the past and improved significantly during these decades – albeit slower than we may have wanted

---

ready to rise to their feet like vicious zombies returning for our brains no matter how many times they have been smitten and laid to rest. A great satire of protectionist theories was written by Frédéric Bastiat in the 1800s and dubbed *The Petition of the Candle-makers*, you can read it online: http://bastiat.org/en/petition.html. It packs a laugh.

[54] Richman, S. L, (1988) *"The Sad Legacy of Ronald Reagan"*, The Free Market 6, no. 10 (October 1988), retrieved from *The Mises Institute* online.

them to be. Rarely did anyone point to the restrictions imposed upon the flow of these markets as the causal factor in perpetuating, for decades longer than necessary, the problems of poverty in the developing world. Once in power, the mainstream right was not about to eat their own by accusing their representatives of not being free market enough. By failing to hold politicians on their side to necessary objective standards, they lost the narrative on free markets in the public mind. The legacy of the Thatcher-Reagan era is that now, more than ever, whatever the socioeconomic problem may be, you can be sure that capitalism will get the blame for it.

Another thing is that people didn't have the same access to information that we enjoy today. Because bad news sells, most assumed that things were getting worse rather than better. They still do.

The figures tell a different story. Despite all the impediments to free trade, foreign meddling, and despotic governments, the percentage of people living in poverty worldwide fell below 10% for the first time in recorded history back in 2015.

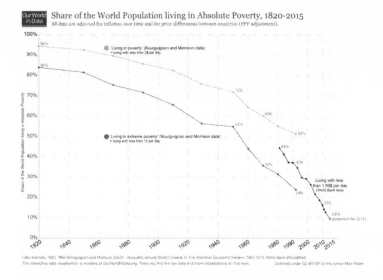

To paraphrase deceased public speaker and statistician Hans Rosling, "138,000 people move out of poverty today could have been the newspaper headline for the last 30 years." Check out some of his cool videos on YouTube whenever you are feeling pessimistic and depressed about the state of the world – they will give you an optimistic kick.[55]

To return to the potential benefits of free trade on domestic affairs, it's interesting to note that fruits and vegetables, which are the building blocks of health, have increased in price faster than other products, while confectioneries have gone down in price in real terms while destroying the quality of life. At the same time, we are forbidden from accepting cheaper fruits

---

[55] You can now get his posthumously published book *Factfulness* which was co-authored by his son and daughter-in-law and recommended for reading by Bill Gates.

and vegetables from the poorest countries in the world in case farmers closer to home might have to find something else to grow instead.

Many worry about the environmental issue of "food miles", or how far food has to travel, but these concerns are misplaced. It is often far more energy efficient to grow foodstuffs in countries with naturally high temperatures than to artificially raise them in colder climates. As Matt Ridley explains in *The Rational Optimist*, only "4% of the lifetime emissions of food is involved in getting it from the farmer to the shops. Ten times as much carbon is emitted in refrigerating British food as in air-freighting it from abroad, and fifty times as much is emitted by the customer travelling to the shops"[56] in their car.

Others worry that development will be an environmental disaster in general, when it's only once countries are developed that they have the wealth to replant forests, clean rivers, defoul water, put recycling infrastructure into place. It's wealth that allows a nation to develop greener alternatives to old-fashioned modes of production. The *World Economic Forum* reported that 90% of the plastic in the ocean arrives there from 10 rivers, eight of which are in Asia, and two of which are in Africa.[57] In places like Bangladesh where people scramble to make a living they have to do so with no

[56] Ridley, M. (2010) *"The Rational Optimist"*, p41.
[57] Gray, A. (2018) *"90% of plastic polluting our oceans comes from just 10 rivers"*, World Economic Forum. Retrieved online: https://www.weforum.org/agenda/2018/06/90-of-plastic-polluting-our-oceans-comes-from-just-10-rivers/

long-term consideration to their surrounding environment, and have no means to repair it afterwards. Similarly, destitute Brazilians have little choice over whether to cut down the rain forest or not when the alternative may be starving. Allowing them to develop their economies by exporting other produce to us will give them – and the planet – another out.

Some on the political right have feared the ascent of developing nations, worrying that they may come to "outcompete" us. These fears are not well founded though. As countries develop, more and more people gain access to higher education and end up working in the service industries and in the development of ideas and inventions rather than manufacturing. They begin to contribute to the intellectual development of mankind. They become capable of inventing things that benefit everyone everywhere. Ourselves included. We all rise together.

This may also lead to environmental benefits. For example, the invention of email, memory cards and flash drives dematerialized the need for millions of filing cabinets full of reams of paper, saving trees. The average smart phone doubles as a camera, radio, television, sound recorder, music player, GPS, flash-light, board and card games, computer games, video player, maps, encyclopaedia, dictionary, compass, photo album, thermometer and scientific calculator.

More innovations of the like are being produced every day. Dean Kamen, an American engineer and businessman, created a water purifier that can purify

1000 litres of water a day using the same amount of energy it takes to power a hair dryer. Over a six-month field trial in Bangladesh the engine was able to run purely on cow dung and provided villagers with enough electricity to charge their phones and power their lights into the bargain.[58] High-tech entrepreneurs are currently working on revolutionary toilets that burn faeces for energy and flash evaporate urine rendering everything sterile. No pipes under the floor, no leach field under the lawn, no sewer systems required to run down the block. Rather than waste anything, these toilets give back packets of urea to be used as fertilizer, table salt, volumes of freshwater, and enough power to charge a mobile phone. If users can sell the energy back into the grid they will literally be being paid to poop![59] So I'm definitely not sh*tting you when I explain, as I did in my article *Misanthropic Myths about 3rd World Poverty debunked!*,[60] that third world development is good for the environment rather than bad! Appropriately handled, international development could turn out to be an environmental boon. We can end world poverty and save the planet at the same time!

By removing all trade barriers, we can help lift millions out of poverty in third-world countries while reducing the price of shopping at home so that those on the

---

[58] Diamandis, P. H. and Kotler, S. (2012) *"Abundance"* Free Press, A Division of Simon and Schuster, Inc., p89-90

[59] Diamandis, P. H. and Kotler, S. (2012) *"Abundance"*, p97-98

[60] Sammeroff, A. (2016) *"Misanthropic Myths about 3rd World Poverty debunked!"* Scottish Libertarian Party. Retrieved online: http://scottishlibertarians.com/thirdworld/.

bottom rungs of the economic ladder here can get their needs met cheaper. It is the least well off who spend the largest percentage of their income on basic essentials, and they are the ones who stand to gain the most from opening up trade with the poorest countries in the world.

In Summary

I've dedicated a third of this short book to outlining several ways of increasing living standards, especially for those at the bottom of the economic ladder, by implementing policies that would radically reduce the cost of living.

You don't need to be in favour of the Universal Basic Income Scheme to see the sense of these economic policies, however, if you *are* in favour of The UBI you *do* need to see the sense of these policies to make it financially feasible any time in the near future.

Without addressing the issues of soaring costs of living precipitated by the undue influence of the central banks over the economy (being allowed to print money and lend it to the taxpayer at a profit, creating price inflation), spiralling house prices, the average working person paying anything from 36 to 48% of their income on various taxes, and high priced products due to over-regulation and restrictions on free trade, the UBI may at best bandage over the bruises for a while. In the long term it may prove untenable unless these issues are redressed.

But What About Automation?

The adoption of machines can result in job losses nominally, in particular industries; but automation does not cause unemployment across the whole economy. Instead, it frees people up to do more productive work, and provides a breadth of benefits that improve the living standards of everyone – especially the poor.

This is the controversial claim I mean to prove before we move on to some final questions and answers.

We are often told that with machines and artificial intelligence, or AI, replacing all the things that regular people do to earn money there will be no jobs left before long. Without employment, we'll all be too poor to buy any of the products the machines are producing – so our only safe bet is to decouple work from a claim on a living by giving everyone a basic income. That way we will all be able to provide for ourselves and actually buy the stuff which the machines are churning out for us.

There is a hidden contradiction in this line of thinking.

The purpose of work is to produce things that satisfy people's wants and needs. If we all actually have everything we want, then there is no work left to be done because the purpose of work is the satisfaction of our desires. However, if people are poor then clearly there is *lots* of work to be done, because they have so many unmet wants and needs. So, there must be jobs so long as there are still people who are poor. The more poor people there are, the more work is needed to make them rich. If rich people have machines that can do that work for cheaper, then all the better, since it is what is done for us that makes us rich rather than what we do for other people (at least materially). If the machines are churning out cheap stuff, then the poor will find their needs met very inexpensively and so will not be poor for very long. They may even start buying things that help them provide for themselves by becoming more productive. Economists call this "capital".

The machines (capital) that are replacing human labour will only be valuable insofar as they can manufacture things that other people not only want, but can afford to buy. If everyone is too poor to buy, then the goods themselves will become worthless. So will the machines that make them. They will take up space in factories and warehouses that have overheads like rent, lighting, heating and electricity. They will become a burden to their rich owners who are losing money by holding onto them and just want rid of them. First, they will try offloading them at knock down rates, then they will offer them for free, then eventually they might have to pay someone to take them off their hands! The robots will end up in the hands of whoever is willing to maintain and upkeep them, or they will be abandoned to a landfill until someone figures out how to recycle them into something useful. Chances are that in a fully automated society, robots themselves will become so affordable that you will be able to buy them for next to nothing to work for *you*.

"That's the long term though!" some will protest. "What about the interim period! It's going to be complete chaos!" Indeed, as the famous economist of the 20th Century John Maynard Keynes put it, "In the long run we are all dead!"

Andrew Yang, author of *The War on Normal People,* a major book advocating the Universal Basic Income as a response to the impending upheaval he predicts will be caused by accelerating automation, warns that self-driving cars are soon tipped to replace millions of jobs. He puts the savings of automated freight delivery at "a staggering $168 billion per year." $35 billion in fuel, $70 billion in labour costs, $36 billion in accident reduction, and $27 billion in increased productivity and equipment utilization.[61] Driven by the profit motive (pardon the pun) the industry is bound to do all it can to realise these savings.

The fallacy is to believe that this money is going to simply evaporate up into the bank accounts of the rich leaving nothing left for 'normal people'. The savings will be reflected in lower prices at the shops, freeing up more change in people's pockets to spend on paying *other people* to do *other things*.

How long we have been told that class sizes are too large in the schools, and getting larger? That hospital waiting lists are longer than ever, and getting longer? That forests have been ravaged and need restoring? That too many elderly people languish alone in their homes, desperate for care and company? That single

[61]Yang, A. (2018) *"The War on Normal People"*, Hachette Books, New York, p44.

mothers have to work three jobs simultaneously and can't get childcare? Meanwhile, most of us cook our own meals, cut our own grass, iron our own clothes, do our own shopping, and a million other things we could outsource if only we had the privilege of great wealth with which to do so.

Clearly there is still plenty of work that needs doing, and no shortage of ways for people to serve one another any time soon. If the truckers need a soft-landing, then surely the most elegant solution would be to simply give *them* a basic income for a year or two after they are made redundant to give them ample time to retrain, and money to do it with. With machines generating a larger and larger percentage of the consumer products we use and the price of them falling as a consequence, a larger and larger percentage of our income will likely be spent on paying one another to fulfil needs that are more people-oriented.

There may come a time when we are so technologically advanced that the moment you think you want a snack you picture it and it will materialise in front of you as though by magic. At that point all manufacturing work really will be obsolete. But there will be no poverty either. Everything will be so abundant that people will just give it away for free. No one will lack anything. It may sound far-fetched but it's already happened with most information, as well as all the music you can get for free on YouTube. Countless eBooks are available to download (including my self-help book *Procrastination Annihilation*), and many regular paperbacks cost next to nothing second hand from eBay. Charity shops can barely get rid of some of the things that people bring in because they are so abundant.

There was a time when buying a new garment would be a great highlight of many people's lives. Now many new clothes items are so cheap that it is not easy to sell clothes second hand. These are often handed on to the needy, demonstrating that surpluses will often be given away freely. The laptops we hold precious today will hardly fetch a price fifty years from now. With 3D printing technology coming along we could find many other things becoming so abundant that they are just given away as well.[62] In the meantime, let's have a proper look at what the effects of automation have been and are likely to continue to be in the short to medium term.

At the risk of sounding tedious, it is often the case in economics that to focus on the immediately conspicuous is to measure a cost which is highly visible, while missing a multitude of benefits which are not so discernible and therefore pass unseen (or vice versa). If someone invents a machine that allows one man to perform the work of two – yes, the second man's job might be displaced – and if that is all we look at we will see the conspicuous loss of a job (or many of them). That said, the workings of the economy at large are far more complex than that, and the net effect of the adoption of the machine will be far more beneficial.

---

[62] I know that people's environmental red lights might be going off here because mine are as well, but the technology can also be turned onto finding more and more efficient ways of using and reusing resources as well as reducing waste.

The detriment is conspicuous because it is concentrated upon a few people. The benefits, while further reaching, are thinly dispersed among the many and therefore inconspicuous, but when aggregated amount to a net benefit.

The *basic economic problem* is that while resources are finite, human wants are actually unlimited. If this isn't true, it's at least approximately true. Whatever situation we find ourselves in we can always imagine a slightly better one, so let's take this for granted as our starting point. We're at least a couple hundred years away from utopia yet.

As human wants are unlimited, advancing technology will allow an economy to produce more products and services that satisfy more people's needs and desires better than before. The employer who buys the machine (that allows one man to perform the work of two) may still keep the second worker on so that he can produce the work of three. On the other hand, if the product he is supplying is already meeting existing demand, he might dismiss the second employee instead. That frees that person up to find work that better serves society's ever-changing needs. Clearly, we don't want people creating things that *aren't* wanted when they can be somewhere else creating things that *are* wanted.

Either way, the product itself will soon fall in price because the costs of production have fallen. If the first capitalist does not reduce the price of it, then someone else will see the opportunity and undercut him to gain a greater market share by getting the same kind of machine and selling the same kind of product cheaper. This means that more people will be able to afford to benefit from the product; and what's more, everyone who could previously afford it at the higher price will have some extra change lying around afterwards to buy something else. That will also create more jobs in other sectors – bringing a higher income to other producers, and the means to employ the worker who may have just been laid off in another industry due to automation. Consumers, who are also employees, give signals to businesses of what to produce, and who to employ doing what, every time they buy something. The fall in prices increases living standards as a whole. Ironically, even the laid off worker benefits from the increase in the purchasing power of the redundancy payment he gets. The freer the economy, the easier it will be to absorb redundant workers into new work, but if there are lots of restrictions on employment and starting businesses it will make it harder for people who lose one job to find another.[63]

Redundancies are not always the result of automation though. It could be that due to falling prices more people buy the product than ever, leading the employer to have to take on *more* staff. Consider how much the demand for cars must have increased once Henry Ford

---

[63] Gene Epstein, former economics editor of Barron's Magazine whom I mentioned earlier, pointed out to me over Skype that while shifts in the economy caused by automation may lead many to think the government must step in and take control, it is actually in areas and times of instability where free enterprise and entrepreneurship are most needed to innovate in response to new challenges.

automated the production line and automobiles suddenly became affordable to the masses. The number of people working in manufacturing had to increase, rather than decrease, to meet the rise. If it doesn't, employment need not be lost on the balance of the whole economy – only in specific places.

Jobs are meanwhile being created in the manufacturing, servicing and maintenance of machines. As economist Johan Norberg, author of *Progress: Ten Reasons to Look Forward to the Future* (2016), put it, "the more machines we have the more people we need to develop them, to manage, and monitor them. It sounds like an unmanned drone is really unmanned, but not really. The US Airforce has concluded that a small MQ1 drone requires a ground crew of 168 personnel. A big surveillance drone relies on 300 people to operate it. And this compares to the 100 people it takes to keep a manned F-16 fighter in the air. And the more data these drones collect the more people are needed to look at this data, monitor it, and reach conclusions. A single drone collects enough video for 20 people to work around the clock to analyse it, and with tens of thousands of drones that's a lot of people." He goes on to state that one General concluded, "The number one manning problem in our air force is manning our unmanned platforms."

Furthermore, machines have created altogether new jobs, and even entire industries, by allowing people to create things that were completely impossible to produce prior to automation. For example, CT Scan Operators and Microchip Assemblers have positions that simply would not have existed without technology. New jobs are being created that couldn't have even been imagined some years ago, and technology will continue to create new fields that we still can't imagine.

Those who fear that automation will concentrate all the money in the hands of the machine-owners do not understand that the economic benefits of automation are automatically distributed to the masses by the mechanisms of the free market itself. The same market forces that push down the price of products after automation are also bound to increase the wages of workers over time because with the use of machines their time is more valuable. If one man is now able to do the work previously done by two, then his labour is twice as productive; and if his employer does not give him an increased portion of the profits (which will have increased due to falling costs of production and selling more units owing to lower prices promoted by machines), then other employers – seeing the opportunity, can enter the sector to take advantage of low labour costs in the industry, offering incrementally higher wages. Raising wages serves the original employer by ensuring he holds onto experienced staff that are already skilled rather than having to hire new employees who may be unproductive at first and require training and experience which may be costly to provide. If production needs fluctuate, then offering experienced workers overtime will usually be preferable to taking on unskilled temps; and making layoffs tends to reduce staff morale which can have a negative effect on productivity. What's more, managers often have a personal relationship with staff and would usually rather not make redundancies if they can be avoided.

Technology is a win-win. When workers are displaced by it, it makes them available to find more productive or specialised work that machines can't do yet. The public is better served because people are now doing things that only people can do, whereas machines are taking up the work that people are no longer necessary to do. Our time is being freed up. In fact, the only reason why most people even have the time and money to enjoy art, culture, science, even a book like this, is because mechanisation has freed up our time. As we discussed earlier, the average work week has fallen from 61 hours in 1870 to around 37 hours today. This is because one person can now do the work that once required several. We have automation to thank for that – in fact if all our machines disappeared today then we would be straight back to working 61 hours a week tomorrow!

Adapting to an economy that is advancing through mechanisation does require of people the ability and willingness to adapt and learn new skills, and that might seem intimidating to some. But, the net result is to actually empower people to take charge of their destiny by becoming flexible, well educated, and multi-talented. It is no longer the time of the industrial revolution where people were defined by their jobs and expected to do those jobs for life, but rather an aspirational time where people can become highly competent in many fields and so be assured that they will always be able to find meaningful work. They can create their own jobs using their skills if they want to. The internet has opened up a near-infinite number of doorways for that.

The education system of an advanced nation should embrace preparing the population for a more creative and dynamic way of living if we are to accept moving towards a highly-mechanised society as a fact of the 21st century. Shifting the focus of education from facts ("what to learn") to methods ("how to learn") would be a good place to start. Nowadays remembering things to write them out in an exam later is not necessarily as valuable a skill as it once was. If we need facts and figures we can find them at the click of a button. A lot of the research for this very book was carried out online. It's more important than ever that people learn how to use information constructively than learn by rote. Critical and creative thinking should play a far more prominent role in the education system. We have been told this is "the era of fake news", and if this is true, then it must be more important than ever that we raise a generation that can tell a valid argument from a fallacious one, and knows how to fact check a document. Creating opportunities for children to practice entrepreneurship and a wide range of practical and vocational skills – as well as allowing voluntary leave from classes for work experience or internships – will help them leave school and enter the workplace, confident in their ability to learn new skills if they ever need to. The masters of their own destiny. Our current education system serves less to prepare our kids to adapt to a highly automated society than to take orders from authoritarian bosses and do what they are told when they are told. But that is a topic for another time.

We can make the best use of the benefits that automation is continuing to shower upon us, if we are prepared to do so. My vision for the future is that machines will continue to replace jobs that are performed by human beings, and things will become cheaper and cheaper to buy. As a consequence, people will have to work less to afford them. The work that remains will be that which requires a human touch. Nursing, childcare, caring for the elderly, helping the disadvantaged, improving people's health and wellness through personal fitness training, physiotherapy, counselling, massage, osteopathic care, yoga tuition, personal development seminars and so forth. Then things that create a more aesthetic experience for others, like waiting on them, performing music, welcoming them to venues and showing them around, cooking for them, and numerous other things we can only imagine. A lot more people will simply spend their time mentoring others one-to-one, or in small groups, to learn very specific skills. Our technological impulse will also be turned towards finding innovative ways of tackling our environmental issues.

As poverty becomes a thing of the past, more and more people will realise that having lots of stuff does not necessarily bring happiness, and this will drive more people to take an interest in personal development, good habits, good health, cultivating fulfilling relationships, creating community, and pursuing creative interests in arts, music, theatre, literature and science. Many people will work in helping others explore and achieve their potential.

Perhaps I'm too optimistic, but this is all possible through automation. Without a UBI, automation will lower the cost of living so people have to work less to meet their basic needs. The main challenge is likely to be delivering people the "soft skills" or "people skills" to be able to meet the demands of an economy that needs them to be there for other people as human beings in their own right rather than to manufacture goods in a factory.

Q&A

Q: Could you elaborate a little on what your vision is in terms of giving people who don't have a sense of purpose, who don't have an incentive ... how can the libertarian view give hope to people and opportunity and purpose to people who might otherwise benefit from the basic income?

A: Well, you have to have a situation where it is lucrative, in my opinion, for employers to train workers. At the moment, there are lots of people who don't have any skills, and they can't get a good job because of that... But it's very difficult to hire and employ people. Many places insist on taking on people who already have experience before they hire them, and so at the very least there has to be minimum wage exemptions for employers who are training their staff. Because, once people have those skills they are completely independent – they can go and take those skills wherever they get the best offer for them, whether it's a lower wage but better conditions, closer to home, or a wage increase and less perks. Higher skills are the road to higher wages.[64] We need to look at how to create a society that cultivates individuals and helps them create opportunities for themselves. That creates a system of interdependence. And when you look at the welfarist models of helping the poor, I am very, very concerned that what we are doing is putting people in a position of permanently relying on unreliable government for their very survival. That is a highly

---

[64] I suggest my article on this subject as it elucidates the crucial arguments regarding what I consider to be a critical topic. Sammeroff, A. (2015) *"Living Wage: The Road to Hell... is paved with good intentions."*, Scottish Libertarian Party. Retrieved online: http://scottishlibertarians.com/living-wage-the-road-to-hell/

precarious predicament. We need to have a society — including radical education reforms — that cultivates individuals so they can get skills and become the masters of their own destiny, and I hope that is a satisfactory answer on that question.

Q: You mentioned about inflation earlier, about quantitative easing — I get that if you print loads and loads of money the value of the money goes down — but the UK is one of the least equal countries in the world. The homes in the South East of England have got 83% more wealth than those in Scotland. So, if we just redistributed wealth more equitably through a progressive system, we wouldn't be adding into the economy and so it wouldn't have an inflationary effect. Related to that, I agree that if when we print money and put it in at the top it's at the highest value when it hits the top, but wouldn't a Basic Income Scheme — even funded by printed money — wouldn't the money have the highest value when it came into the hands of the poorest.

A: Thank you those are excellent questions. So first of all, it's a great thought, print the money and give it to the people at the bottom to circumvent the problems of it being issued from the top. The thing is you are going to get price inflation much faster that way. Because there is a flood of money, shop owners and landlords are likely to just hike the prices up immediately. The other problem is you're not giving those people the means... I mean... What you are doing when you redistribute the wealth is you go to the deep end of the swimming pool, then you've got some bureaucracy over here (politicians, tax collectors, office workers and what have you) so you spill some on the way, you put it in the shallow end – those people go out spending it in the shops and it flows back to the rich people again. It's not durable. So, what you need to do, in the interest of creating a more equitable society, is even out the depth of the swimming pool. You need to give these poor people at the bottom *capital*. And I don't just mean machines and factories, I mean skills; the ability to acquire their own wealth. So that the money doesn't just all flow to the 1% when they go to the shops and spend it. You need to build up the personal capital of the poor, so that they can become creators in themselves, and then we have a more equal society. I hope that is helpful to you. [applause] Thank you.

I should add, redistributive policies have never ended poverty anywhere. The United States, for instance, has spent nearly $15 trillion on welfare since President Lyndon Johnson declared a "war on poverty" in 1964.[65] In 2012, the federal government spent $668 billion on 126 separate anti-poverty programs. State and local governments added another $284 billion, bringing the total to nearly a trillion, amounting to $20,610 for every poor man, woman and child in The States.[66] Bearing in mind that the US has a tiny proportion of the world's

[65] Free Market Foundation (2018) *"Media release: Oxfam's latest report is dangerous and intellectually dishonest"*, retrieved online: http://www.freemarketfoundation.com/Article-View/oxfam-cares-more-about-ideology-than-poverty.

[66] Tanner, M. (2014) *"War on Poverty at 50 — Despite Trillions Spent, Poverty Won"* Cato Institute, retrieved online: https://www.cato.org/publications/commentary/war-poverty-50-despite-trillions-spent-poverty-won

poor, all US poverty should have disappeared long ago if redistribution actually corrected the problem.

When you redistribute money nothing new is created in the process that will actually increase productivity or living standards. However – when the "greedy rich" invest their money in businesses those businesses buy factories and machines which increase productivity and increases supply of goods, making them more affordable to everyone. This benefits the poor the most, which is why so many items that were once considered a luxury (such as a personal computer or smart phone) are the norm – even in poor households in the west. This is not an argument for 'trickle down' economics – the idea that if you let a few people at the top grow very wealthy then they will buy machines, and the people who sell the machines will employ people to make them, who will then go out to the shops with their wages, and so on. It's simply an application of the law of supply and demand which says the more "stuff" there is knocking around, the cheaper that "stuff" will be. And it's supported by the empirical evidence of our senses. As I've discussed most of what we buy is so much cheaper than it has ever been in the past. A pineapple once cost the equivalent of thousands of pounds. Now you get one in the supermarket for 67p and think nothing of the fact you are enjoying an exotic luxury.

I may be making myself unpopular here when I say I'm not for redistribution as a method of tackling inequality, but I didn't invent these facts I am just reporting them. I'm also against the government redistributing wealth from the bottom to the top by giving handouts and special privileges to big business and the rich as well, and we are seeing plenty of that.[67] So much wealth is being drained out of the economy and given to those who are politically connected, I don't mean by tax avoidance but by actual government handouts from the public purse to big business. It would be a good idea to start there because it would not only put money back in the hands of people who worked for it, but it would focus companies on doing their job – which is to create products and serve customers, rather than create busy work and lobby government.

Ultimately, when it comes to helping the poor, I maintain that you are on firmer ground empowering people to generate their own wealth rather than to redistribute that which we already have. I feel it's the most humanitarian solution as it doesn't leave anyone in the precarious position of being unable to put food on their own table should the 'helping hand' of government be suddenly withdrawn.

(The following question was asked by the same

---

[67] In my article *The Excesses of Capitalism* I report that: "According to The Sunlight Foundation for each of the 5.8 billion dollars spent by America's 200 most politically active corporations between 2007 and 2012 on federal lobbying and campaign contributions, they got $741 in return in kickbacks and benefits. To pay for these kickbacks tax-payers were left $4.3 trillion dollars poorer - but that's not all. $5.8 billion was spent in political gaming instead of invested in jobs and product development. These incentives drive companies to misallocate resources by making products that the general public doesn't want profitable, and products that they do unprofitable. In other words, the government has become the client of these corporations rather than their customers." You can see the full article here: www.therationalrise.com/the-excesses-of-capitalism/

questioner, but I was not able to take it into account in my original response as I was short of time and focussed on responding to his first two. I have included a fresh response here.)

Q: The final bit is that if incomes do go up in accordance with your suggestions, then demand for goods would also go up and economics 101 is that when demand goes up prices go up, wouldn't the price of everything go up to track the increase in incomes resulting from your policies?

A: It's true that if incomes go up then prices will go up – on the condition that the supply of goods remains the same as it is now. Retailers would happily increase their prices to take advantage of the increase in incomes, given the opportunity. All of us would also love to get higher wages for doing the job we do. However, we can't necessarily just accost our boss at will and demand a higher wage. Particularly if there are droves of other people willing to do the same work as us for the same money as we are getting. Similarly, outlets can't charge much more than anyone else is charging for similar products or people will just shop elsewhere. Other companies will undercut them, and people will shop there instead. As the profit margin of any product or service increases it serves as an incentive to entice more entrepreneurs into that industry to take advantage of a high return on their investment. The choice of consumers (you and I) to opt for the best value product at the best price from a choice of potential suppliers will drive prices down and profit margins back to regular levels. The government can intervene to halt this process by granting special privileges to the big boys, disbarring all but a few suppliers from operating in the relevant market, or offering patents, but I am against all that. It's important that people understand that bosses don't choose what to pay their staff or what to charge for products. Prices are arrived at by supply and demand. You can't pay someone less than someone else is willing to pay them, and you can't charge someone more for something than someone else is willing to charge them.

Q: What is your overall view on the UBI?
A: On one level I love the idea of everyone's needs being met, but I can't ignore the fact that policies have unintended consequences and that I don't think implementing a UBI would have the consequences that its advocates hope for. That's why I have focussed my efforts on trying to demonstrate how we can actually meet everyone's needs by giving them more liberty. The goals of the UBI's proponents will be reached through automation if the market is allowed to function, because it will bring the price of everything down so low that people can acquire it for themselves without being put in a dependent position. This process will take place faster the more we allow the market to function uninhibited, but preferential treatment by government towards big business, restrictions on who can and cannot do business, and patent laws may slow down the process. You can discuss policies for making sure workers who are displaced by automation are taken care of while they find new work, but these would have to be surgical if you want to avoid creating more welfare traps.

Q: Do you see any benefits of the UBI over the present system though?

A: Yes, the biggest benefit is that it could potentially end the poverty trap and remove welfare cliffs where if people out of work earn more, they take home less. Loss of benefits act like an additional tax on work, meaning the poor are burdened with the highest effective tax rate should they attempt to work their way out of poverty. Often if people put in more than 16 hours or earn more their benefits will be cut and they will take away less – this discourages them from finding meaningful work and integrating into society. The state also wastes huge sums of the money collected for the poor on bureaucracy and busy work. That is the second biggest benefit. It would potentially be cheaper to administrate.

Q: And are there any advantages of the current system over the UBI then?

A: Yes. At least it is discriminatory. You're not giving a handout to people who are so rich that they don't need it. Perhaps more importantly, you're not potentially just giving a large sum of money each month to people who don't know how to manage it and will waste it or spend it badly. You're not necessarily giving out the cash straight to individuals with substance addictions, gambling problems or bad spending habits which get them in trouble. You're not necessarily giving a handout to people who are addicted to computer games and Facebook who might benefit from getting out to work in a bar or cafe and mingling with the public for some occupational therapy. In many cases with the UBI you would actually not be helping people. You'd be making their lives worse. You'd be making their deaths worse. They will end up not being able to get up off the couch without assistance – or the toilet seat when they get old – because of their sedentary habits. It will be disempowering and humiliating, and we are doing nothing to prevent it from happening. We need to get everyone doing exercises like squats from a school age. I'm sorry to be graphic but these are not trivial issues, they are important and they have to be considered.

Q: Is it not fundamentally unlibertarian of you to judge what uses of the UBI are worthy and which are not?
A: I don't think so. According to libertarianism how you spend your own money is your business, that is true. But how you spend other people's money is definitely their business. When you add negative consequences that most people would not support it makes it much worse. Handing a suicidal person a bottle of sleeping pills might not be identical to murdering them, but it's still highly questionable morally. Add to that you took the sleeping pills away from someone else who might really need them. Likewise, you have to be a pretty callous person to say "Well, it's their life, they've got a right to ruin it. Let them take out their UBI and spend it on hard drugs if they want to." Now I suppose the common-sense response is to say, "Well people with problems can be vetted and asked to attend clinics to receive their UBI," but where do you draw the line? What about people who have addictions to bad food or don't take any exercise? Are we not back to a towering bureaucracy to decide who is and isn't eligible and can sanction people to save the government money? This is something that people are complaining about with

regards to the present system already.

Q: You mentioned in your "for" section that the UBI might help alleviate stress and other mental health issues because people would have more security. Is that not a view you actually share in? Leading Economist Guy Standing often speaks of the emancipatory value of a basic income, for example, what do you understand this to suggest?

A: That may very well be so in the short term, however, it will certainly not remain the case if the UBI is weaponized by the government to threaten people with benefits sanctions for not behaving as the government of the time sees fit. These people will be in a far worse position, particularly if the fact that they have been receiving a basic income for a long time has led them not to pursue economic skills or to lose the ones they already have because they have not needed to use them. They will be completely at the mercy of the state under the threat of poverty or even starvation because they have no hope of being able to provide for themselves or their families. This would make the basis of a good dystopian science fiction novel, but sadly I'm only too convinced that this is what would end up happening if those in power were in charge of everyone's purse strings.

There is nothing emancipatory about being dependent on a handout. The only thing that is emancipatory is helping people learn skills that are useful to other people, because if you can provide value to others they will be willing to provide value back to you and therefore with or without a basic income you will have reason to feel secure.

Q: I'm also a libertarian, but I think most of your criticisms of the UBI more accurately apply to the present system. You may have successfully debunked giving everyone a universal *generous* income that supports a luxurious lifestyle but have not debunked a Universal BASIC Income that provides a safety net. If there was no welfare state these would be good arguments for not adopting one in the form of a UBI in the first place.

At the moment with the tax credit system, people are encouraged to stay in low paid jobs or work part time. If you work or earn more you lose the credit, so what is the point of taking on more work or responsibility? Someone who works but loses their job and owns a house loses their house, but someone who has never worked can get their rent paid. At the moment working people who buy property upsize throughout their lives and downsize later in life. People on benefits expect the state to provide a house for life. The bedroom tax tried to tackle this and in Scotland and failed. There is no motivation to work. Our current system rewards laziness and poor lifestyle choices, such as having children you can't afford and then not living with the partner. With a basic income these will have to be paid for out of the basic income. No extra money. It's the current system that has people dependent on the state for a living. It's the current system that is unsustainable. I don't see an alternative to the UBI for weaning people off the welfare state. The House of Lords has overruled welfare cuts in the past.

The cost of any increase in basic income would be immediately transparent. We have shut down departments like ATOS, the job centre, the CSA and various others. How could it possibly make "the poor" any more of a political weapon than they already are? This is what we mean by decreasing bureaucracy. Take for example things the left promises, such as free child care places, free school meals, free prescriptions. All they will have in their arsenal is to offer an increase in basic income.

A: If I am understanding you correctly your argument is that the UBI will be able to replace all sorts of systems that we currently have now and reduce the size of government, and that therefore it is a favourable policy from a libertarian (small government) standpoint. My problem with that argument is that assumes *ceteris paribus* – that all other things will stay the same.

I don't see a compelling reason to believe that the UBI will be the end of it. It's only so long after it's been instituted that people start saying this group or that group should be earning a higher basic income. To take your example, we have had a child, we need a higher basic income. I am a single mother, I need a higher basic income. Then people will advocate for a higher UBI for the elderly, disabled, people who live in areas where the rents and costs of living are high, or where they have to travel long distances to work, and so on, ad infinitum. On the face of it the argument will sound quite compelling. I mean, why *shouldn't* vulnerable groups and those who have to pay more to live get a supplement? It's only fair, right? But then we are back to the problem of towering admin costs to see who is due what and checking that people aren't abusing the system. Any group which represents a large enough voting block can influence the government to add supplements to their basic income, and (coming back to public choice theory) there is no compelling reason for any administration not to cater to them to buy votes. This way we will soon lose all the supposed benefits of the basic income in terms of doing away with complex bureaucracies. If we are to do away with poverty trap, maybe it's best to just institute a rule that for every one pound or dollar you earn you only lose half that in benefits. That creates a graduated system that does away with welfare cliffs. It would also require administration, but it would probably solve more problems than it creates. I don't think anyone is saying that the present system should continue to go on without any reforms whatsoever.

Q: So, what do you think would actually happen if the UBI scheme was instituted here in the UK?
A: To be honest I think there's a good chance that the pound would just collapse in value because people would want money that is worth something because it corresponds to actual human labour. I mean, websites have already been created that will offer to pay you their own cryptocurrency, let's call them shmekels, they will pay you 100 shmekels a day. There's your basic income. The problem is the shmekels aren't worth anything because they're issued for free. They don't represent any sacrifice on the part of anyone else, whether in the form of hard labour, or deferring consumption to invest. I think there's a good chance

that people would just start trading with euros or dollars or bitcoin or Ethereum, and pounds would just become interchangeable with monopoly money. I think the money would be worthless so it would be a complete failure. Who knows what would happen after that. Some radical futurists are probably rubbing their hands with glee at the idea of bitcoin taking over, but people do not react well to chaos. The collapse of the currency could result in people rioting, it could end in a police state.

Q: What are your views on the current benefits system, including what you believe to be its benefits or failures?
A: Not popular. I think it's done at least as much harm as good. Before there was a welfare state in this country there was an organic network of friendly societies and unions as well as churches and charities that formed the basis of a welfare system where people were engaged in their community and looked after one another. That was when society was far less wealthy than it is now. Poverty was already on a steep decline. If someone lost their job, their union or friendly society might support them financially and even help them find a new one. They had a direct incentive to find something suitable for them sooner rather than later in order to keep dues down, and since they couldn't compel anyone to be a member and pay into the system they would have to demonstrate that this would be a worthwhile thing to do. Had this organic system, built from the ground up rather than imposed from the top down, continued, then coverage would have been immeasurably better now than it was in the past. All the new wealth, technology, and the adoption of best

practices arrived at through trial-and-error over time would have been channelled into optimising these sorts of grass-roots safety-nets which are of, for and by the people – and cement community. The welfare state supplanted that network, trapping many people in intergenerational welfare dependency.

We often hear that we live in an atomised society now, where no one knows their neighbours. I fear this is in part because the government has stepped in to fulfil the role that community used to fulfil, except for without a face. Local institutions can organize community projects to help local people help one another, or produce revenue. They have the information on the ground and a direct insight into the needs of the people in front of them. They can provide counselling, offer care in the community and training in whatever skills are needed to help people lift themselves out of poverty. The state has assimilated the function of these institutions and done a worse job. Because states do not have the facts on the ground in local communities they cannot provide intricate and specific solutions tailored to the needs of people in poverty, so they provide a "hand out" rather than a "hand up." They spend the money they appropriate through the tax system very inefficiently. Only a small percentage of it reaches the hands of the people they are supposed to be helping. I am not simply taking a mercenary view on this – wasting public funds that are meant to go to helping the poor is not just a crime against the taxpayer, it is a crime against the people who need that money the most.

As you can see from the following chart, poverty was steeply on the decline in the USA *before* the big government welfare programs began in the late 60s under president Lyndon B. Johnson. This decline levelled off, and despite some fluctuations, has stayed more or less constant since then.

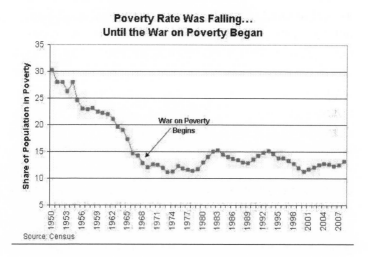

If we want to enter conspiracy theory territory, we could argue that the state stands to gain from as many people as possible being dependent upon it for their income because these are essentially captive voters. If there was no poverty and no social problems (most of which poverty plays a factor in fomenting) the role of the state would decline. I am not saying this was deliberately engineered, but every system tends to produce the results which it is incentivised to create. Even while people within the system are working very diligently to do good, the system as a whole tends in the direction the wind is blowing it.

Relying on voluntary institutions may seem precarious, but the benefit of charitable giving over the tax system is that you can compare the performance across different bodies to see who is doing the most with a little. You can donate to the organisation that is doing the best job. That is the purpose of the *Effective Altruism* movement, to offer good information on how to make your contributions go the longest way. If Government was on the league tables it might come out at the bottom. A friend of mine who raised money for charitable causes said The Red Cross, one of the least efficient charities, still managed to get around 45% of donations to the people they were supposed to be helping. The government in the UK only manages around a third.

Most Western countries give between 0.5 and 2% of their GDP to charity, with America by far being the most generous. With the policies I have suggested the cost of living would be so low that those in work would have more to contribute and those out of work would require less to meet their needs. People would be richer as well and have far more to spare. Help in the community would be focussed on providing those people with opportunities and skills so they could become autonomous and make their own living, where possible. In fact, it would have to be, because charities are limited in resources. They can't keep people in a condition where they are reliant upon them forever the way governments can.

Q: Are you saying you would abolish the welfare state then?

A: No, because that will not solve the problems that it has created. If you build a ship around the assumption that you need a central beam for it to stay afloat, the ship will sink without it. Someone with vision could come along and say, 'Hey, I could build a ship without that central beam! Instead it will have ribbing all along its sides. The ship will be more efficient, faster, stronger at most angles, durable, and will have more cargo space!'. People might think this person is crazy until they see the new design in action, then they will soon accept it and wonder what people were ever thinking to doubt that this would be possible. The central beam in this analogy is government obviously, while the ribbing is 'society.' Grass-roots organisations, community projects, social enterprise, local businesses, charities, NGOs, and what have you. As we have acknowledged, our central beam is beginning to look pretty ragged and unsustainable. If we are wise, we will start to build our ribbing now before it collapses completely. That means we need to institute the policies that I have suggested in my section on *Meeting Everyone's Needs* so the cost of living comes down far enough, and others to bring down the price of provision for education, healthcare and anything else we can. Then we need to phase out welfare programs in such a way that the third sector can step in to replace them as they go. With the political will you could use targeted tax breaks to incentivise the change, but to be honest it's unlikely because you're basically asking the dragon to slay itself and cough up the treasure. Politicians will not stand to gain from instituting these policies until they are vote-winners. People like me who advocate for them will be slandered as heartless neo-liberals who must just hate the poor, when actually I stand nothing to gain from advancing unpopular opinions. I just share the truth to the best of my knowledge and that is not always politically correct. The truth will set you free, but first it might annoy you.

Q: As there are now a large proportion of citizens working precariously on zero-hour contracts or in the unreliable service industry, do you not think a basic income would give them a safety net?

A: For those who don't know, a zero-hour contract is a type of contract between an employer and a worker where the employer is not obliged to provide any minimum working hours, while the worker is not obliged to accept any work offered. Some argue these create an unfair power imbalance since an employer could choose to sanction an employee for not taking undesirable hours by not to offering them any further hours at all. Zero-hour contacts *can* be advantageous to people like students, tradesmen who work "on call", parents who are a secondary breadwinner, and the elderly, who might all appreciate the flexibility. However, critics say that they put too many people in a precarious position because they can't predict how many hours or how much money they are going to get from one week to the next.

I think it's important that people come to understand that zero-hour contracts are not motivated by the desire of employers to exploit their workers, but by the desire to get around the complex array of labour laws that make it difficult to make hiring someone profitable. No business is going to employ someone who is going to lose them money and that's that. We don't typically go around paying for things which we don't believe will give us more in use value than we pay for them either, that's just good sense. There's nothing wrong with businesses not employing people that will cost more to hire than they will generate in revenue either. It means people don't waste resources paying people to make x when there is no public demand for x. They will employ them to do y, which there is a public demand for, instead. It's so hard to get people to understand that when the government passes a law to "help workers" they can't really know what will serve "workers" the best. Employees needs and preferences will differ so radically from one sector of the economy to another that no one-size-fits-all law can possibly be sensible. That means public officials have to make a "best guess" which will only help some people but will probably hinder many others because they have to pay for the cost of compliance with regulation, in part, out of their pay-checks. Labour laws cannot increase the actual value of people's labour to the public, which is what ultimately determines the pay and conditions of work.

Employers have a certain amount of money to budget for their labour costs and it makes no difference to them whether they spend it directly on their employees' salaries, health insurance, a nicer staff room, a gym on the premises, free pony rides – or anything else. That means if the employees would prefer an extra 15-minute tea break over a pay-rise they would actually be likely to get it. If the government mandates the 15-minute tea break instead, most people will believe that they are getting it in addition to their pay, but it is actually instead of it. Preferences that differ so widely from one place to another cannot possibly be accounted for by a team of government bureaucrats in London or Washington, only by the market.

I may have strayed somewhat off topic but these are exactly the kinds of misconceptions I am desperate to confront so thank you for the question. To answer more directly, it could help them in the short term. The rest depends entirely on how they spent their free time and money. If they invest it in building skills that are helpful to others, then they will have a bright future. If they don't, they will still be in a precarious position because a sudden change in policy could leave them in the same position they started in or an even worse one.

Q: A lot of your arguments appear to be based on models and predictions, but there are some studies that you can check your hypotheses against. You seem to be concerned about runaway price inflation, but in an Indian experiment the costs of some goods actually went down, and in the Namibian UBI experiment self-employment went up 301%. UBI increases access to capital, and it reduces the risk of people trying out business ideas.

A: Ah yeah. Unfortunately, those studies are a really dubious source of evidence for at least a couple of reasons. The first is that the money to provide the basic incomes for those people is taken from *outside* the relevant population.[68] So for example, if we took one valuable item from each of your neighbours' houses and put it in your living room once a month and documented your living standards over a period we wouldn't be surprised to see them increase dramatically. However, in the meantime your neighbours are getting poorer! These studies can't be considered relevant to say instituting a UBI in the UK because the revenue would be raised from taxing the same population, not bringing money in from the outside. The whole point of a UBI is that there is no outside to bring money into, its universal.

The second reason is that the people taking part in these trials knew ahead that they were only receiving the money for a short period, rather than indefinitely, and so they were more likely to save it or invest it wisely. If someone offered us a one-time large sum of money, we would be far more likely to use it wisely than if they promised to keep it coming each week for the rest of our lives. Imagine that. Maybe we'd just get drunk and party for the first week to celebrate, then the next week we'd recover on the couch watching Netflix. Sounds like a good time! We'd plan on getting around to doing something constructive with our money eventually, but we wouldn't be under any time pressure to do so because we could always blow this week's payment on more fun and promise to be more responsible next week. We don't necessarily value what

---

[68] For more, see: Schneider, H. (2017) *"Universal Basic Income – Empty Dreams of Paradise"*, ZBW – Leibniz Information Centre for Economics. It's available online:
https://www.ceps.eu/system/files/IEForum22017_4.pdf.

we don't have to sacrifice for (say, by working.)

Now, you might argue that not everyone is like you and I in this scenario. Party animals who like nothing more than chilling out watching Netflix on a hungover Sunday. But that only goes to prove my point. One of the major issues with the UBI is that it's non-discriminatory. Why *should* people who are just going to use it to party get it *at the expense* of people who are working their butts off, while there are other people who actually would use the money to improve themselves and others? Shouldn't we at least award it fairly? I'm afraid I think these studies have mostly been reported on by utopians who are in love with the ideal of the UBI and its promise of freeing everyone from worry and poverty. Those are worthy goals and I myself am very dedicated to the elimination of poverty as you have seen from my alternative proposals, but unfortunately good intentions do not determine the outcomes of policies – the laws of economics do. It's an important point you raise though. What do we make of the evidence?

In Finland's recent experiment with a basic income they found that people loved being given free money (who wouldn't?) but they were unable to decrease unemployment or increase self-employment for the 2,000 lucky recipients who received €560 a month between January 2017 until December 2018. What it is impossible for these studies to measure is the cost to everyone who was taxed to fund the experiment and what the benefits would have been of them spending the money themselves if it were not taken from them.

Also, regarding your second point on the UBI reducing the risk of people investing in businesses... I don't mean to be pernickety, but we can't assume that reducing the risk of investment is universally a good thing. Risk plays an economic function to discourage people from wasting resources on creating things that no one actually wants. From an economic perspective, investors are there to act as qualified judges of what ideas are likely to be successful and what ideas aren't. They put their wealth on the line to back ideas they think might be successful. If they do a bad job of it, they lose their capital. They have skin in the game and don't want to lose their money, so they have a strong incentive to gather all the necessary information together and make well-informed decisions on what businesses to invest it in. Investors with a good eye for a smart innovation will gain more resources to steward. That's as it should be, because ultimately the public (you and I) determine what investments will be successful and what won't be when we choose what to buy. The investors job is to guess what we want. Now, people taking risks and trying things out is great, but with their own time and money, because everything has an opportunity cost. Any resources that are misallocated by the UBI to ill-conceived pet projects could have actually been going to fund something that would have really helped people. We shouldn't ignore this side effect if we are concerned with people's welfare, because it's most significant. I wish more people understood these concepts because they are relatively simple. There is no such thing as a free lunch, well-intentioned policies can have poor results, and every economic decision comes at the expense of every other possible decision that could have been made instead. There is no perfect decision-making process because humans are fallible, but some systems have more fail-safes than others.

Q: What would you do with your basic income?
A: I would probably do the same thing I'm doing. I like being in personal development and writing about economics. But I would probably take more trips and holidays and go on more trainings and self-help events to get better at what I do. Might be jetting off to some economics conferences as well – don't judge me.

Q: So you would use it to build up your "personal capital" as you advise others to do? What if the government only gave handouts to people who wanted to train and get more skills so they could get a higher wage then?
A: It's a tempting idea, but the result would likely be lots of trainings opening up that weren't actually useful because people would be trying to take advantage of the free money. Remember the government already had each of us for 11-13 years in school and in all that time they didn't teach us anything that would fetch twice the minimum wage, even though that is long enough to train to be a concert pianist, so why would you trust them to fund the right training? You already hear of lots of "hobby" degrees in things like *The Beatles* – you can do it at one British university and out of the public purse. To be sure there is nothing wrong with pursuing your interest in The Beatles, that's what we are all ultimately here to do, pursue our interests,

but out of your own pocket – it's wrong to force others to pay for you to do it. Especially when there is an opportunity cost. That is then money which is *not* going to help someone who is actually in dire need. On a free market, employers would pay to educate their employees because the employers themselves stand to gain from having a well-trained workforce. They can charge more for the services of well-trained staff than staff that can't do the job properly. Why should the taxpayer take the burden of capitalists to provide training? Again "local institutions have the facts on the ground" – they know what is needed. Government officials and even universities – sometimes even trade schools – cannot see what the immediate needs of a worker is to the customer. That's why whatever good you try to do through government will likely be corrupted, however well intentioned.

Postscript:
UBI – Utopian Dream or Dystopian Nightmare?

This essay is based on a talk I gave at the Eighth International Conference of the Austrian School of Economics in Vienna on November 14th, 2019.

I'm sitting in the pub after a *Skeptics Society* meetup. I don't go very often, but there was a famous author speaking, and living in a bit of a social media bubble (as most of us do these days) it's a rare opportunity for me to get a window into what thinking people outside my circle have to say on some of the issues of the day. A warm chat ensues over a pint with a couple of the other attendees when miraculously the conversation at my table turns to the *Universal Basic Income.* My neighbour gushes with vigour over its merits. He eagerly vows that it will solve innumerable problems facing our civilisation, and I get the feeling he has been spreading the gospel at every available turn because this idea is the crucial one. If only he can get enough people to believe it...

I abstain from mentioning my book as I don't want to prejudice his answers to any of my questions. Besides, once I start talking I've got a habit of not being able to shut up. Best keep my big ideas to myself, right? I politely wait my turn, and then ask a simple question:

"What do you think the potential disadvantages of the Basic Income would be, then?"

He replies, "There aren't any."

Economists have heated disagreements on just about every issue under the sun. But there is actually one point they are all probably unanimous on. That is the fact that every policy has winners and losers. Given that human wants are infinite, but our means towards attaining those wants are limited, policies – by their very nature – advantage some groups at the expense of others.

The *Universal Basic Income* seems unaffected. It's going to cure poverty, eliminate stress, reduce crime, unleash entrepreneurship, emancipate women, save us from AI, and even fight climate change. I'm not exaggerating. I googled, and there are multiple articles claiming that, not only will the UBI save the economy from flatlining due to a lack of consumer demand by increasing consumption, but somehow also put a halt to global warming as well – contradictory as these two aims may seem.

Is the UBI is a Flying Unicorn that poops rainbows?

Perhaps so. Perhaps the laws of economics will suspend around the good intentions of its advocates. Such is the strength and cavalier of their idealism.

Maybe I'm being a little harsh on budding idealists though. After all, this lad doesn't have a background in economics, does he? He's just looking for an easy way to save the world! Surely, I should pick on someone my own size. *Professional* advocates of the UBI are bound to be more even-handed in their consideration of the program, and present a more nuanced view of its comparative advantages and disadvantages, aren't they?

Well, not according to the titles of their books...

Rutger Bregman comes right out and calls his book advocating the UBI: "Utopia for Realists"

Annie Lowrey's book "Give People Money" Carries the subtitle: "How a Universal Basic Income Would End Poverty, Revolutionize Work, and Remake the World."

Andy Stern and Lee Kravitz book, "Raising the Floor.", carries a subtitle claiming the UBI will, "Renew Our Economy and Rebuild the American Dream."

Phillipe Van Parijs and Yannick Vanderborght entitle their book: "Basic Income: A Radical Proposal for a Free Society and a Sane Economy."

This boundless idealism scares me. The Russians were also offered utopia after the Tsars, as were the Chinese when Mao came to power. If I deviate from my so-far ecumenical tone in this new coda, please forgive me. It's partially because people seem to readily forget what the road to hell is paved with.[69]

Most people agree that politics is a dirty game, and that political powers will inevitably be used to further the agenda of officeholders and their cronies. That said,

---

[69] Need I add *The Road to Serfdom*, for that matter.

despite being immersed in the current thinking regarding the UBI for three years now, I have seen precious little worrying as to how the government might finally exercise power over everyone's purse strings once they had seized control of them.

This is the same class of people launched a permanent war in the middle east wasting trillions of dollars on destroying millions of lives. They bailed out the banks from the public purse and gave themselves raises after telling the rest of the nation we had to tighten our belts. They have robbed the young of the opportunity to own a home by sending house prices through the roof, and mean to leave them a nation in ruinous debt. They continue to lock away huge numbers of people (sometimes for decades) on what amount to victimless charges, leaving their children to be raised single-handedly. They have created an oligopoly of higher education provision forcing generations into student debts that cannot be defaulted on; and healthcare systems so restrictive that people must pay inordinate sums to get care, or be forced onto government waiting lists so long that their conditions are often chronic or untreatable by the time they get seen to.

Am I the only one who thinks the power to give (and withhold) a UBI may one day also be used for evil rather than good?

If we take a look across to China, where they are instituting a "Social Credit System", we might glean some insight into what may be in store for us around the corner with the application of the UBI.

Under the *Chinese Social Credit System* the government judges their citizens behaviour and trustworthiness in order to give them a rating out of 1000 which officials can then improve or dock. If people play their music too loud, don't pay a court bill, owe the government money, or are caught jaywalking, for example, they can lose certain rights such as booking flights or train tickets. The government can have their internet speed throttled, or exclude them from getting the best jobs. They can be banned from the best hotels. Their children may be refused the best schools. They may be publicly named and shamed as "bad citizens" – or even have their dog taken away. This is literal tyranny. Rule by fear.

Now a Basic Income Guarantee may begin universal, but as the years wear on and it proves expensive to grant, corners may be cut to ensure its continuance. Hardly anyone will object to the UBI being withdrawn from criminals, for example. And then perhaps for anti-social behaviour. Petty crimes, like littering the street, might lead people to receive a penalty against their UBI. A few might moan that this is the beginning of a government social-engineering program, but to most people it will seem like a quite a sensible and reasonable measure. After all, we all "benefit" from the benevolence of society providing our roads and schools, and now our Basic Income. So, if some choose to repay society with vulgar behaviour such as spitting in public, throwing the ends of cigarettes, failing to remove their dog foul, or what have you... why should society continue to furnish them with the fullness of a basic income? Besides, once they receive the fine, they are very unlikely to repeat the crime. They will soon learn their lesson. We will save money on law enforcement, lengthy court trials, and prison sentences – all of which are costly. Clipping people's Basic Income will soon seem the most sensible and appropriate response to many crimes and misdemeanours.

People may soon be penalised for things like not sorting out their recycling. After all, the government provides garbage disposal for us, and the environment is at stake. Many governments are already looking at sanctioning people for this kind of behaviour, so it would be the next logical step. These moves will simply be designed to acclimatise people to the idea of being "nudged" in the right direction before more radical measures are taken to use the UBI to shape their behaviour.

In China, people can have their Social Credit Score docked for buying too many video games. Under the UBI, there are bound to be complaints that some people are taking advantage of the system but not paying in. Detractors will preach that misusers are damaging themselves as well as society. It will therefore seem sensible, and compassionate, to save money while encouraging people into better habits by docking their UBI if they spend too much time playing on the computer on clicking around on social media. The government will likely have many bright ideas as to what kind of activities they should be getting up to instead. Soon there will not be rewards for "good" behaviour such as contributing to charity, or volunteering time. But how long can such a system remain impartial? How long before people start creating malignant causes to launder and take advantage of free government money? How long before the government starts to select which behaviours and causes are worthy and which are not? Lobbying and campaign contributions will soon become necessary to have causes approved. The government rewarding specific activities with public funds supplants the market system with a "bribocracy" where people can climb the ladder – not by directly providing goods and services that others are willing to pay for – but by finding out what the government approves of and collecting brownie points. If spying on neighbours and reporting their so-defined "anti-social" behaviour qualifies for rewards, it will not be the first time a government has called upon its citizens to tell on one another. Sycophants will find lucrative roles and the servile will be elevated to a privileged class while independent minds are castigated for non-conformity.

In China people can have their social credit score docked for posting fake news online. We may, of course ask, fake according to whom? After all, the Chinese government maintains that the Tiananmen Square Massacre of 1989 was "fake news" drummed up by the west to undermine the regime. Closer to home, the mainstream media was entirely complicit in selling the war on Iraq to the public, but I very much doubt we will see punishments for posting news from BBC or MSNBC. Are our leaders above falsifying our historic records and sending embarrassing incidents down the memory hole for permanent deletion?

The purse strings of the Universal Basic Income also present a grave threat to freedom of speech. Anyone who has been following the "woke wars" on twitter and other social media platforms will have heard of people receiving lifetime bans for tweeting things like "men are never women." Now whether you believe such a statement is transphobic or otherwise, you might at least believe that someone has the right to tweet it, and be duly educated as to their wrong-doing by other users. The Universal Basic Income could easily become the new weapon to wield against those who hold unpopular opinions or those that are simply no longer politically correct. It will be first used to strike against unpopular groups such as racists, misogynists, homophobes and bigots. Not many people will come to their defence when they lose their Basic Income for spreading hate. But one day you yourself may hold an unpopular opinion that is relatively benign. Maybe you will say that people shouldn't have their Basic Income docked just because they say unpopular things on the internet. You will not just be slapped with a twitter ban; but potentially lose $1000 a month.

Conservative, Charles Murray, states in *Losing Ground*, his book advocating the UBI, that it would require people to have a "universal passport" and "known bank account." I don't think it's unrealistic to imagine that people may soon be forced to accept a mandatory Government ID Card in order to claim their Basic Income. Before long they will be asked to show it in order to get into government buildings. Then at the airport to get on a plane. Then simply to board a train or a bus. Then to post a package. Then to get into a bar.

Then a restaurant. Before long every public place will ask you to show your ID Card. If a policeman asks you to identify yourself you will be expected to produce it, and failure to comply might result in a penalty to your UBI. You'll certainly need to produce it in order to vote, and before long *not* voting may result in a fine as well. In a time of war, you may be expected to enlist in the military or risk losing your UBI for denying your patriotic duty. Just as states freeze the assets of suspected fraudsters, they will soon be freezing the "known bank account" of political dissidents. By the time they come for those with radical ideas about freedom from government tyranny there will be precious few left to speak out for us.

Far from creating a futuristic utopia where – once our security needs are met – we are all liberated to pursue our dreams, become great scientists, scholars, artists and entrepreneurs, the universal basic income threatens a totalitarian horror the likes of which we are used to seeing imagined only on *The Twilight Zone* and *The Outer Limits*.

Certainly, the poor, who depend solely on their handouts to survive, will quickly become very cautious of what they say and do. But even reasonably affluent people will think twice before risking the money. The UBI institutionalises the state as patron, and citizen as ward. Before long we may arrive in a frightening era where payments and penalties are used to mould us into compliant little drones. The utopian dream will have descended into a tyrannical nightmare.

Afterword *by Dominic Frisby*

Well, I enjoyed reading that. Thanks very much Antony.

I first met Antony Sammeroff at the Edinburgh Festival in 2016, when he and Tam Laird came to see my show *Let's Talk About Tax*. The next day I went to his flat in Leith to record an interview for the *Scottish Liberty Podcast*. What struck me about Antony is not only how passionate he is about his libertarian beliefs, but how well read and versed he is on the core arguments. What's more he is an uncompromising purist.

Because libertarians believe in small government, they tend to be branded "right wing" and, as we all know, right wing people are, without exception, evil and bad and don't care a fig about anyone's welfare. Anyone who has met Antony knows what a warm and gentle person there is lurking beneath the cold, absolute libertarian exterior.

Antony is at the forefront of what I call "Bleeding Heart Libertarians". The impossible message they have to get across is that less is actually more when it comes to government intervention in the economy. For all the good intentions behind the Welfare State, it has trapped people. For all the good intentions behind the NHS, it is not the best means to provide the best possible healthcare to the most amount of people at the lowest possible price. There are always unintended consequences. The paradox is that if you want the needy looked after, a large, interventionist state is not the best means to do that. But anyone who stands up and says, "we are going to help you by doing nothing" has an almost impossible argument to win.

I came to this book generally believing in UBI for the simple reason that it is better and simpler than what we currently have. To go straight from large state Britain to a libertarian anarchic ideal is too big a jump in practice. UBI could be a bridge. What really stimulated me about Antony's argument is the sheer cost of UBI. Where is the money going to come from? As soon as you have free money – money created without labour – as Antony rightly points out, you undermine its value. Fiat money (currency without intrinsic value that has been established as money, often by government regulation) is doomed anyway. And with the successive devaluations that have gone on its days are numbered. If crypto-currency is not sufficiently evolved by the time fiat dies, there is going to be a painful crisis. UBI could well be the pin that bursts the fiat bubble. That's a danger.

Ultimately, I think Antony's right in his purist approach. The reality, however, is that the State is here to stay and that UBI in some form or other is inevitable. Thus, it is doubly important we are aware of its potential shortcomings.

Dominic Frisby
Author of *Bitcoin: The Future of Money?* (2014)
and *Life After the State* (2013)
March 13th, 2018

Additional Resources by Yours Truly

Writing this book was a lot of fun because it gave me the opportunity to draw upon a wide range of research and writing I had done earlier and pull the strands together like a nebula forming into a star. I think expanding upon my UBI talk made for a far more interesting end product (god, I sound like an economist) than a simple collection of essays would have. I have endeavoured to bring my writing and speaking together in a *Best Of* (to continue my "band-on-a-reunion-tour" analogy from the introduction) in one place, before building upon it with *unique bonus material*. I think the result makes a good stand-alone piece, however, if you can't get enough of my writing (you're only human after all) or would like to see where the book all began (as far back as 10 years ago!) I have prepared a list of "clickable" links to all of the previous articles, YouTube videos and podcasts that I drew upon when creating *Universal Basic Income – For and Against.*

You can access at: www.therationalrise.com/ubilinks

I hope you will enjoy.

Bibliography and Recommended Reading

• Ayittey, B. N. (1997) *"Africa in Chaos"*, Macmillan Press Ltd.

• Bastiat, F. (1845) *"Economic Sophisms"*, public domain.

• Caplan, B. (2007) *"The Myth of the Rational Voter"*, Princeton University Press.

• Diamandis, P. H. and Kotler, S. (2012) *"Abundance: The Future Is Better Than You Think"*, Free Press.

• DiLorenzo, T. J. (2016) *"The Problem with Socialism"*, Regnery Publishing.

• Frisby, D. (2013) *"Life After the State"*, Unbound.

• McCloskey, D. N. (2016) *"Bourgeois Equality: How Ideas, Not Capital or Institutions, Enriched the World"*, University of Chicago Press.

• McCusker, J. J. (1991) *"How Much Is That in Real Money? A Historical Price Index for Use as a Deflator of Money Values in the Economy of the United States"*, Amer Antiquarian Society.

• Norberg, J. (2016) *"Progress: Ten Reasons to Look Forward to the Future"*, Oneworld Publications.

• Pinker, S. (2018) *"Enlightenment Now: The Case for Reason, Science, Humanism, and Progress"*, Allen Lane.

• Ridley, M. (2010) *"The Rational Optimist"*, Fourth Estate.

• Rosling, H. (2019) *"Factfulness: Ten Reasons We're Wrong About The World - And Why Things Are Better Than You Think"*, Sceptre.

• Sammeroff, A. (2018) *"Procrastination Annihilation"*, Rational Rise Press.

Acknowledgements

I would like to thank all the libertarians who came out to support me when I originally gave this talk including Abe, Alan, John, Scott and anyone else I have forgotten, sorry :(. Thanks to Tom Laird for being my 'friend' and hosting the *Scottish Liberty Podcast* with me which has given me plenty of opportunities to get better at articulating complicated economic themes to a lay audience. I like to be comprehensive and all-embracing in my approach, and he sits through my rants, often with genuine curiosity which helps a lot. He also contributes humour (sometimes interrupting me in the process, grrr) to what would often otherwise be dry subject matter from my end.

Thanks to Davie and Alan for pushing me to speak at the event, and to Johnny Cypher for having me and giving me a big hug after my talk. Thanks to my brother Jonathan for his encouraging feedback on the presentation as well as additional proofreading on this eBook. Thanks to the people who commented on some of my YouTube podcasts arguing in favour of the UBI as I assimilated their questions and arguments into the Q&A. Thanks to Ross Buchanan for providing additional questions, and to Katrina for pointing out the flaws in one of my arguments about the effects of quantitative easing so I could fix it. Thanks to Peter for working tirelessly behind the scenes for the Scottish Libertarian Party, and his support of my writing and additional thoughts. Thanks to Stevie and Stef for their hard work and good humour. Thanks to Daniel for always attending meet-ups. Thanks to Derek for being one of our earliest fans and helping Tam and I with audio on occasion. Thanks to Abe for describing me (accurately) as a "f*cking legend" (you might have forgot that one sonny, but I will never.) Thank you to Tom Woods who had me on his show multiple times following this talk and helped expose me and my podcast to a far larger audience than I would have been able to reach without his support.

I have to extend special gratitude to Bob (Robert P.) Murphy for taking time out of his busy schedule, not only to write me a foreword, but to give me extensive feedback. Our email exchange felt like I was receiving private tutelage from a master. He helped me eliminate fallacies, and pushed me to be more rigorous with my evidence where my work was not sufficiently annotated. Same to Dominic Frisby for phoning me straight after reading the draft to express his enthusiasm for the project and agreeing to contribute an afterword. Dominic also was a sport, letting me steal one of his jokes. In his show *Let's Talk About Tax* (Edinburgh Fringe, 2016) he asked the audience "What is the most expensive thing which you will ever buy?" to which they all responded, "a house!" Dominic was one jump ahead and said, "If you said a house, you were wrong. Actually, it's government." This witty sleight of hand worked as well in my talk as in his show, and I hope it also provoked a chuckle from you while you were reading.

Thanks to James Fox Higgins at *The Rational Rise* for eagerly syndicating my articles to his website and asking to make this little eBook into a paperback.

Extra special thanks to Chelsea Ellen for offering her proofreading skills once again, and to Rufus Terris for spotting not less than 42 errors among my revisions – enough to push me to put out this 2020 edition. As always, any remaining mistakes are most assuredly down to my own pig-headed stubbornness with my style rather than any oversights on their part.

Thanks to Gene Epstein at *The Soho Forum* for his additional support, passionate feedback on the text, as well as proofreading on my automation section which he was very complimentary about. I look forwards to my appearance at his debating society in the new year.

Thanks to Timothy Virkkala, for kindly volunteering to creating the cover for this book and going to great lengths to make sure I was satisfied with it. Images are not my strong point, but he was able to take the idea and make it work. Thank you!

Thanks to some special friends who had me on their shows to talk about my ideas: Sherry Voluntary, Danilo Cuellar, Pete Raymond, Marc Clair, Richard Cox, Johnny Adams, Kyle Anzalone, Bennett Hunter, Steven Clyde, Jeremy Henggeler, Mike Maharrey, Nick and Lizzie Pecone, Daniel Elwood and Robert Johnson, Tony Rockamora and Jeff Invalid Beard, John Coleman, Scotty D Luffy, Trey Weaver, Mike Tilden, Riley Blake Patrick MacFarlane and any others I have missed.

I want to thank all of the genuine and kind-hearted left-wingers and UBI-Supporters who gave me not just a fair hearing – but a warm reception at their event; not to mention an uproarious round of applause, even though I was advocating a position which was, at times, directly opposed to their own.

Last but not least as they say, I would like to thank you for reading my short book, especially if you are in favour of the Universal Basic Income Scheme. I have huge appreciation for people who expose themselves to arguments against their view. I hope I have provided you with value and opened your mind up to at least one thing you did not know about before taking the time to read it. I hope you will consider including some of my suggestions on central banking, tax and regulations, housing, and free trade in your advocacy from now on.

Warmly,

Antony Sammeroff.

PS. Download my free self-help book *Procrastination Annihilation* at www.beyourselfandloveit.com/doit

PPS. Feedback to this email address: capitalismmisconceived@gmail.com. I can't always reply to everything I receive but I would love to hear your thoughts, arguments, questions, what you liked/disliked, and if there is anything I have missed that I shouldn't have.

About the Author

Antony Sammeroff lives in Glasgow, Scotland where he loves the people but hates the cold. He writes the blog *Seeing the Unseen – The Art of Economics* and co-hosts the Scottish Liberty Podcast along with Tom Laird, which you can subscribe to on YouTube, iTunes and Soundcloud. His articles have been published by The Mises Institute, The Foundation for Economic Education, The Scottish Libertarian Party, The Cobden Centre, The Backbencher, The Rational Rise, and ActualAnarchy.com to name a few.

Antony has also appeared as a guest on several podcasts to discuss libertarian ideas including the popular *Tom Woods Show*, *School Sucks Podcast* with Brett Vienotte, *Lions of Liberty* with Marc Clair, *Free Man Beyond the Wall* with Pete Raymond and many more.

He has interviewed many prominent thinkers and writers including popular YouTuber Stefan Molyneux, leading candidate for the 2008 Libertarian Party presidential nomination – Mary Ruwart, activist and author Adam Kokesh, economist Nima Sanandaji – author of *Scandinavian Unexceptional* and *Debunking*

Utopia, economist George Reisman – author of *The Government Against the Economy* and *Capitalism: A Treatise on Economics*, foreign-policy expert Scott Horton of antiwar.com, expert on the Israel-Palestine conflict Dr. Norman Finkelstein, world-leading scholar of anarchism Keith Preston of attackthesystem.com, historian, political theorist and author Sean Gabb, author, comedian and voice actor Dominic Frisby – author of *Life After the State*, Darren Loki McGarvey – rapper and author of *Poverty Safari*, documentary film-maker Colin Gunn, historian Thomas E. Woods, economics writer and liberty advocate Jeffrey Tucker, philosopher Dr. David Kelley of *The Atlas Society,* sociologist and author of *The Rise of Victimhood Culture,* Jason Manning.

Besides economics and political liberty, Antony's other great passion is personal development. At the beginning of 2018 he published the free self-help book *Procrastination Annihilation*. You can download it from beyourselfandloveit.com/doit. He hosts the *Be Yourself and Love It!* Podcast weekly, which you can subscribe to on iTunes or Soundcloud. The podcast shares practical information to help people improve their lives in all areas including physical health, diet, relationships, dating, mental health, parenting, communication skills, productivity, income, work-life-balance and so on. He also regularly posts short live-streams to YouTube on various self-help related topics.

You can find Antony's Professional Website at:
www.beyourselfandloveit.com